MYTHS & LEGENDS
OF BRITAIN
& IRELAND

MYTHS & LEGENDS OF
BRITAIN &

RICHARD JONES
Photography by JOHN MASON

NEW HOLLAND

IRELAND

This edition first published in 2006 by New Holland Publishers (UK) Ltd
London • Cape Town • Sydney • Auckland
www.newhollandpublishers.com

10 9 8 7 6 5 4 3 2 1

Garfield House, 86–88 Edgware Road, London W2 2EA,
United Kingdom

80 McKenzie Street, Cape Town 8001,
South Africa

Level 1/Unit 4, 14 Aquatic Drive, Frenchs Forest, NSW 2086,
Australia

218 Lake Road, Northcote, Auckland,
New Zealand

First published in 2003 by New Holland Publishers (UK) Ltd
Copyright © 2003 in text: Richard Jones
Copyright © 2003 in photographs: John Mason and other
photographers as credited on page 160
Copyright © 2003 in maps: © MAPS IN MINUTES™ 2001.
© Crown Copyright, Ordnance Survey & Ordnance Survey
Northern Ireland 2001 Permit No. NI 1675 & © Government of
Ireland, Ordnance Survey Ireland.
Copyright © 2003, 2006 New Holland Publishers (UK) Ltd

ISBN 10: 1 84537 594 7
ISBN 13: 978 1 84537 594 2

Publishing Manager: Jo Hemmings
Project Editor: Lorna Sharrock
Editorial Assistant: Gareth Jones
Copy Editor: Sue Viccars
Designer: Alan Marshall
Assistant Designer: Gulen Shevki
Cartographer: Bill Smuts
Index: Janet Dudley
Production: Joan Woodroffe

Page 1: Rock of Cashel
Pages 2–3: Giant's Causeway
Pages 4–5: Chanctonbury Ring
Pages 6–7: Main picture: Stiperstones; From left to right:
Dunvegan Castle, Wayland's Smithy, St Govan's Chapel,
Kilpeck Church
Pages 156–7: Glastonbury Abbey
Page 160: Chalice Well at Glastonbury

Reproduction by Pica Digital Ptd Ltd, Singapore
Printed and bound in Singapore by Kyodo Printing Co
(Singapore) Ptd Ltd

Of Gods and Other Men

I shall tell you tales of heroes
And gods who walked as men.
On mountains where the wild wind blows
or across the darkling fen.
I shall tell you tales that minstrels told
Of vengeful queens and warriors bold
Of kings who sleep and ne'er grow old
In caves their dreams residing.

I shall tell you tales of outlaws
and hounds that roam the night.
Of secret realms through hidden doors
Where ancient giants fight.
I shall tell you tales of long-lost lands
Buried now 'neath shifting sands
Where dancing maids have long held hands
In stone their spirits writhing.

RICHARD JONES

CONTENTS

INTRODUCTION

In 225BC, at the battle of Cape Telaman on the Italian sea coast, the legions of the Roman Empire inflicted a crushing defeat upon an army assembled by a group of peoples that history has chosen to remember collectively as 'the Celts'. Those who survived the decimation faced stark choices. Some attempted to negotiate a settlement with their Roman oppressors; others fled east, settling in Asia Minor where they established their state of Galatia. The majority headed west, and large numbers reached a mysterious place that the Romans had named the Pretanic, or Tin, Islands: the area that would eventually become Britain. Those early Celtic settlers assimilated the beliefs and culture of the aboriginal population into their own poems, stories and folk tales, which they duly adapted to their new habitat. Thus was born a tradition of story-telling that, because of the islands' turbulent history, has been consistently added to and revised ever since. Each new invader and settler — be they Roman, Saxon, Angle, Jute, Dane or Viking — would mix their own beliefs and traditions with those of previous cultures.

One invader, however, has had a far more lasting impact on British and Irish folklore than all the others put together and, furthermore, came armed with a book rather than a sword. This invader was Christianity, and its exponents realized that, if their message was to be accepted by the natives, then it must absorb rather than annihilate cherished beliefs and customs. Wells and springs, which the Celts had held sacred for thousands of years, became 'holy wells', and Christian saints soon replaced the 'pagan' gods that were believed to dwell beneath and beyond their waters. Whatever wonders were said to have occurred around them were eclipsed by the miraculous actions of these saints. Celtic feasts became 'holy' or 'saint's' days, and Christian churches suddenly began to flourish on sites that the Celts had held sacred since time immemorial. Again, in order to demonstrate the superior power of the new God, these foundations were often imbued with fantastical and supernatural origins. Meanwhile, the heroes of native mythologies either metamorphosed into Christian saints, or else found themselves demonized.

More importantly, Christian monks did something that the Celts had never done. They wrote all this down, and so their *literary* tradition, although absorbing pagan elements, was given a bias and interpretation that ultimately eclipsed the Celtic *oral* tradition. Only in Ireland, which was Christianized much earlier than Britain, and where the ancient Celtic sagas were viewed as entertaining rather than religious, were the Gaelic myth cycles and story-telling traditions allowed to survive in a relatively unadulterated form. Over the centuries that followed this oral tradition would continue to evolve

RIGHT: When visiting the Roman baths in the city of Bath, conjure up an image of the Goddess Sul Minerva, who was the deity to whom the Romans dedicated these hot springs.

ABOVE: Britain's most mythical monarch, King Arthur, is presented with Excalibur by the hand of the lady of the lake, whilst Merlin looks on.

OPPOSITE: Rockfleet Castle, once the home of Ireland's legendary pirate queen Granuaile, who as a girl dressed in boy's clothing to get taken onboard ships.

as it absorbed influences from successive waves of invaders — Angles, Saxons, Vikings, Danes and Normans.

Then, in the 15th century, the development of printing both revolutionized and, ultimately, stunted oral traditions' growth. Up until then a saga or tale may have been recorded in manuscript form somewhere, but minstrels, bards and storytellers took it to a wider audience. They, of course, would add their own particular slant to the narrative and localize it to include places and characters with which their listeners could empathize. Printers, on the other hand, would gather together the many different facets of particular tales and piece them together into one narrative. Over a period of several hundred years, the art of storytelling moved from the spoken to the written word as authors, historians, poets and playwrights began condensing a wide variety of, often contradictory, traditions into one *definitive* version. In the process a distinction became apparent between myths and legends: myths became a record of events that were supposed to have happened in the distant, almost ethereal past, whilst legends began to focus on one particular figure or location.

And so it has continued down the ages. By the 18th and 19th centuries most of the well-known myths and legends — such as those of King Arthur, Robin Hood and Lady Godiva — had arrived at the form in which they would be handed down to us. True, the likes of Sir Walter Scott might have tampered with them slightly, but the basic characters and narrative have remained static. Meanwhile, new legendary figures such as Dick Turpin and Jack the Ripper have entered the national consciousness and evolved in much the same way as their predecessors, by absorbing other traditions and using spurious facts to form cohesive narrative and so arrive at a definitive version that we know today.

I have been asked one question more than any other during my researches, and that is 'What is the difference between a myth and a legend?' It is a difficult one to answer, since the line dividing the two is often blurred. I can only say that, in my opinion, the secret of a good myth is that it must make you suspend belief, whilst the secret of a good legend is that it must make you believe in it.

Richard Jones

When I set out for Lyonnesse,
A hundred miles away,
The rime was on the spray,
And starlight lit my lonesomeness
When I set out for Lyonnesse
A hundred miles away.

When I came back from Lyonnesse
With magic in my eyes,
All marked with mute surmise
My radiance rare and fathomless
When I came back from Lyonnesse
With magic in my eyes!

FROM *WHEN I SET OUT FOR LYONNESSE*
BY THOMAS HARDY (1840–1928)

FABLED LANDS
and GOLDEN SHORES:
ARTHUR'S
MYSTERIOUS
KINGDOM

CORNWALL, DEVON & SOMERSET

A fantastical aura of mystery and magic hangs heavy over England's West Country. Tradition says that from the sea-sprayed cliffs and tumbling granite of Land's End, the lost kingdom of Lyonesse once stretched. As you travel through the timeless villages of the eerily beautiful Cornish countryside, the spirit of Arthur, that most legendary of British kings, haunts a landscape of ruined castles, ancient hill forts and enchanted pools. To the north-east, the wilderness of Dartmoor, with its sinister tales of hellish hounds, gives way to the rolling green fields of Somerset, where the Holy Grail is reputedly buried and where, on the fabled Isle of Avalon, King Arthur is said to rest. Add to all this an abundance of brooding stone circles and prehistoric remnants, and you have a potent brew of tangible history around which myth and legend have woven a tapestry of wonder that remains as vibrant today as ever it was in the past.

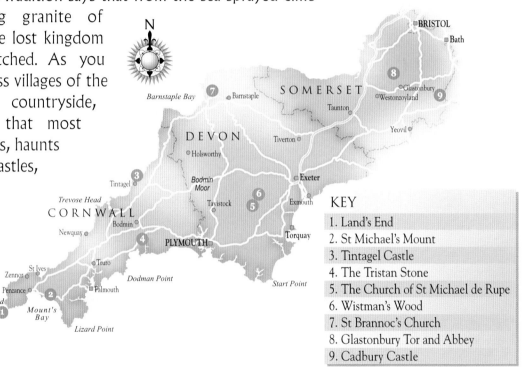

KEY

1. Land's End
2. St Michael's Mount
3. Tintagel Castle
4. The Tristan Stone
5. The Church of St Michael de Rupe
6. Wistman's Wood
7. St Brannoc's Church
8. Glastonbury Tor and Abbey
9. Cadbury Castle

LAND'S END
The Lost Kingdom of Lyonesse and the Death of Arthur
LAND'S END, CORNWALL

Charles Dickens claimed that he knew of no experience equal to that of watching a sunset over Land's End, and although the place has changed since his day, it still possesses a magic, which the paraphernalia of the tourist industry cannot dispel. Take a few short steps to the east or west and you encounter some of the most awe-inspiring clifftop scenery in Britain. Stand here on a still summer's day, when a silvery tide fills the myriad coves and inlets below, and feelings of genuine enchantment wash over you. Return to the very same spot when a belligerent westerly is whipping the waves into a foaming frenzy, or a white mist covers the rugged headland, and you sense the awesome majesty and changeable temperament of the place.

Legend has it that a lost kingdom – Lyonesse – lies beneath the emerald waters that stretch from this jagged coastline to the Isles of Scilly, 45 kilometres (28 miles) to the west. It was a fabled land of splendid towns, ripe orchards and 140 churches. One of its inhabitants, a man named Trevelyan, became concerned at the, apparently, dangerous inroads that the sea was making against the land, and moved his family and cattle to higher ground. His fears proved well founded; one day a great flood swept over the kingdom, drowning everyone except Trevelyan who, having leapt onto

PREVIOUS PAGES: An air of enchantment hangs over the offshore islet of St Michael's Mount, where a hideous giant once lurked in a gloomy lair.

ABOVE: The lost Kingdom of Lyonesse is said to lie deep beneath the sea that stretches from beneath the rugged cliffs of Land's End.

his white horse, galloped before the waves and managed to reach the safety of a cliff cave at Land's End. In the past, local fishermen are said to have frequently dredged up masonry and panes of ancient glass in their nets, whilst others say that on storm-tossed nights the bells of the lost land can be heard tolling beneath the waves.

The Arthurian epics claimed that this lost land was the Kingdom of Lyonesse where Tristan, the famed lover of Iseult, was born (see page 18). In Tennyson's *Idylls of the King*, it was in 'the sunset bound of Lyonnesse', in the fading light of the winter solstice, that Arthur fought his final battle against Mordred. A 'death-white mist slept over sand and sea', causing such confusion that 'friend slew friend not knowing whom he slew.' Arthur's faithful knights fell around him and then, at twilight, a dead hush fell. Suddenly, a bitter wind blew the mist aside to reveal Mordred standing amongst the corpses, Arthur rushed at him, but was smitten 'hard on that helm which many a heathen sword had beaten thin.' With one last stroke of Excalibur Arthur managed to kill Mordred, but then he too fell, fatally wounded.

BELOW: During Arthur's last battle, in the fading light of a winter solstice, Arthur kills his nephew, Mordred, but is fatally wounded himself in the process.

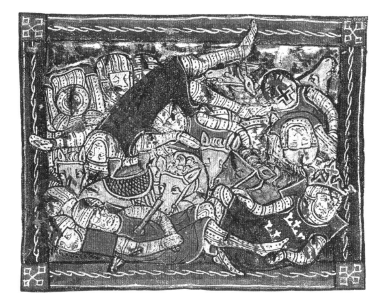

St Michael's Mount
Jack the Giant Killer
MOUNT'S BAY, CORNWALL

Rising from the sparkling waters of one of England's prettiest bays, St Michael's Mount is a rocky jewel whose magic slowly draws you across its sea-sprayed causeway. Tradition holds that the island was once the eastern border of Lyonesse, whilst legend maintains that King Arthur once battled a ferocious giant on its shoreline. It is, however, the Mount's association with another mythical figure that has transcended the centuries to be recounted time and again in storybooks the world over.

Tales of Jack the Giant Killer have swirled around the eerily beautiful Cornish coastline for centuries. In his earliest incarnation Jack was a popular folk hero who came to St Michael's Mount to rid the region of the scourge of the unruly giant, Cormoran. This hideous creature, whose fierce and savage aspect was the terror of the district, stood 5.5 metres (18 feet) tall and 1 metre (3 feet) round. Each night he would leave his gloomy lair on top of the rock and wade across the bay to plunder the cattle of his neighbours on the mainland.

One evening Jack swam to the Mount

> **'You saucy villain, you shall pay dearly for breaking my rest, I shall broil you for my breakfast.'**
>
> CORMORAN THE GIANT THREATENS JACK

ABOVE: The mysterious sea-sprayed ruins at Tintagel, where King Arthur was conceived by Uther and Ygerna, as a result of Merlin's trickery.

OPPOSITE: Mystery and enchantment swirl around the 16th-century castle atop St Michael's Mount, which legend declares was once the eastern border of Lyonesse.

and dug a deep pit, which he covered with bracken, sticks and earth. The trap set, he waited till dawn, and then blew loudly on his horn to rouse the sleeping colossus. Cormoran raced angrily towards him, bellowing, 'You saucy villain, you shall pay dearly for breaking my rest, I shall broil you for my breakfast.' Moments later the ground gave way and the astonished Cormoran tumbled headlong into the pit, where Jack finished him off with his pickaxe. When the justices of Cornwall heard of the giant's defeat, they declared that Jack should ever after be known as 'Jack the Giant Killer'.

Tintagel Castle
Arthur's Conception
TINTAGEL, CORNWALL

Only ragged vestiges now survive of this once-mighty fortress. Its sullen grey walls cling tenaciously to a clifftop that has been almost broken in two by the interminable assault of the roaring ocean beneath.

It has been suggested that it was the foundation stone for a much older structure that once stood here, and the similarity between 'Artognou' and 'Arthur' is, to say the least, intriguing.

For the thousands of visitors who each year make the exhausting climb to the ruins, proof is unimportant. For them this is a place where history and fable can exist side by side, and where the magic of Merlin, coupled with the powerful imagery of Arthur, instils a sense of timeless wonder.

THE TRISTAN STONE
The Story of Tristan and Iseult
NR FOWEY, CORNWALL

This 2.1-metre (7-foot) tall, weather-beaten monolith stands by the side of the road between Castle Dore and Fowey, and is said to have once marked the grave of Tristan, nephew of King Mark of Cornwall. Tristan's love for Iseult is one of the greatest romances ever told, and has provided heart-rending inspiration for writers and poets for centuries.

When King Mark refused to pay his annual tribute to his overlord (the King of Ireland), the latter sent his brother-in-law Marhaus to Cornwall to demand payment. Tristan, however, slew this colossal Irishman, but received a poisoned wound in the process. None of the court physicians could cure him, so Tristan placed his trust in Providence and headed out to sea in a boat with neither sails nor oars.

Eventually the vessel washed up on the Irish coast, where the king's beautiful daughter, Iseult the Fair, nursed him back to health. Tristan kept his identity secret lest he be recognized as the slayer of her uncle. His strength restored, Tristan bade her farewell and headed back to Cornwall, where the barons were demanding that Mark should marry and beget an heir. One day, two nesting swallows flew past Mark's window and dropped a long strand of golden hair at his feet. The king told his barons that he would only marry the maiden to whom the hair belonged. Tristan recognized it as Iseult's, and promised to fetch her.

He found Ireland being terrorized by a fierce dragon, which he killed, and the grateful king offered him his daughter's hand in marriage in return for this good deed. Tristan, however, remained true to his uncle and took Iseult with him to Cornwall, but on the way the couple accidently shared a love potion intended for the newly-weds on their wedding night. They fell hopelessly in love and, although the royal marriage went ahead, Tristan and Iseult remained secret lovers. The jealous barons ensured that word of his wife's adultery reached Mark and the lovers fled into the forest where, despite their poverty, they lived in great happiness for three years before the potion wore off. They decided that Iseult should return to her husband.

Mark, however, would only accept her back if she swore over the bones of a saint that she had never been unfaithful. To this end, the royal retinue headed for church. Tristan, who

ABOVE: The discovery of the 'Artognou Stone' at Tintagel in 1998 excited the world of Arthurian belief because of its Latin inscription, implying links with Arthur.

Although the present structure dates from the 13th century, tradition has bestowed a much older and illustrious pedigree upon these sombre ruins, claiming them as the place where King Arthur was conceived. One Easter a great feast was held at the court of King Uther Pendragon and among those who attended was Gorlois, Duke of Cornwall, whose wife, Ygerna, was considered one of the great beauties of the age. When Uther set eyes on her he was smitten, and made his feelings so obvious that Gorlois took his wife back to Cornwall and locked her inside his castle at Tintagel.

Uther besieged the castle, and, when it proved impregnable, sought the assistance of his mentor, Merlin, who used his magic to make Uther resemble Gorlois. In this guise he was admitted into the castle where Ygerna, thinking he was her husband, spent the night with him and Arthur was conceived. The next day Gorlois was killed in battle and Ygerna agreed to marry Uther, thus legitimizing their unborn child and making him heir to the throne.

Historians are very much divided as to whether Arthur actually existed and, if he did, whether he ever set foot here. In 1998, however, the discovery of the 'Artognou stone' on the site sent waves of excitement rippling through the world of Arthurian belief. Its 6th-century Latin inscription translates as 'Artognou father of a descendent of Col made this.'

had disguised himself as a leper, met them en route and offered to carry the queen over a river. Iseult climbed onto his back and thus, when she took the sacred oath, was able to swear that no man had ever been between her thighs except King Mark and the leper.

Tristan decided that he owed it to Iseult to go overseas where, after many adventures, he settled down and took a Breton bride, Iseult of the White Hands. One day Tristan was mortally wounded in battle and, with the physicians unable to help, he sent for Iseult the Fair, hoping she would again cure him. He told his messenger that upon the ship's return he must hoist a white flag if Iseult was on board, and a black one if she had refused to come to his aid. Tristan was at the point of death when the vessel hove into view and he asked his wife what colours it was flying. She lied that the boat was showing a black ensign, whereupon Tristan let out a cry of despair and expired. When Iseult the Fair arrived and found him dead, she too collapsed in sorrow and died.

Tristan's body was brought back to Cornwall, where this poignant monument, so legend says, once marked his grave. Although it is unlikely that Tristan ever lay beneath it, no one who gazes upon its sullen countenance can deny that it casts a sorrowful and truly regal aura.

THE CHURCH OF ST MICHAEL DE RUPE
The Tempest-tossed Merchant
BRENT TOR, DEVON

In 1625, Tristram Risdon wrote that St Michael de Rupe (meaning 'of the rock') was 'a church, full bleak, and weather-beaten, all alone, as if it were forsaken', and his description has never been bettered. The church is 334 metres (1,100 feet) above sea level, and the rocky crag on which it stands may once have

ABOVE: The Tristan Stone, which reputedly marks the burial place of the fabled lover of Iseult the Fair, daughter of the King of Ireland.

RIGHT: The church of St Michael de Rupe is a beacon for miles around and may commemorate the divine and miraculous rescue of a wealthy merchant, caught in a storm at sea.

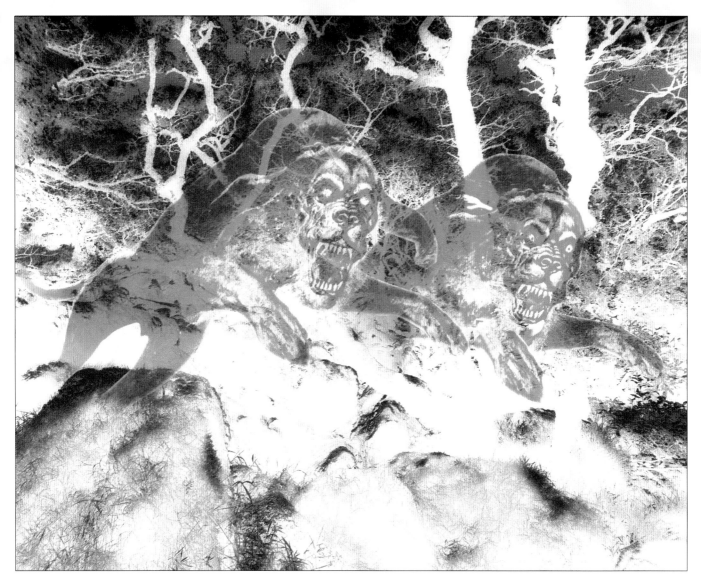

been part of a volcanic cone. The first church here appears to have been built around 1130 by Robert Giffard, whose father, the Lord of Longueville, came to England with the Norman Conquest. Legend, however, says that the church was built by a wealthy merchant, whose ship was caught in a storm off the south Devon coast. In the midst of the tempest he cried out to his patron, St Michael, that if he were saved he would build a church upon the first land he sighted. Whether Brent Tor could have been the first land he saw is debatable, but the legend is an established part of local folklore and was repeated by Charles Kingsley in *Westward Ho!*, first published in 1855.

WISTMAN'S WOOD
The Devil's Wisht Hounds
NR TWO BRIDGES, DARTMOOR, DEVON

Situated amidst the bleak terrain of Dartmoor's wildest reaches, eerie Wistman's Wood is an ancient and haunting copse of wind-gnarled oaks among a tumble of moss-covered

ABOVE: The eerie atmosphere of Wistman's Wood can be overpowering, especially when the fearsome and dreaded wisht hounds venture forth to hunt for souls.

boulders. It is believed locally that the feared and fearsome wisht hounds are kennelled beneath its gloomy canopy. When the wild storms of winter howl with demented fury across the moor, these spectral black hounds are said to come baying from the depths of the wood to join the Devil as he seeks out the souls of unbaptized infants or chases lone wayfarers to their deaths into the mires and bogs that litter the moor.

An old tale tells of a farmer who was once riding home from Widecombe Fair when the pack of hounds, urged on by a dark huntsman, hurtled past him. He called out, asking how the hunt had gone, and wondering if he might share some of the game. 'Take that,' boomed a sinister voice, and tossed him a large bundle. Picking up the gift, with a mixture of trepidation and excitement, the farmer hurried home, eager to open his bounty. On unwrapping the bundle, however, he discovered that it contained the body of his own infant son.

St Brannoc's Church
St Brannoc and the Animals
BRAUNTON, DEVON

This delightful church possesses many interesting features, including numerous carvings depicting the miracles of its founder, St Brannoc, a 6th-century missionary who is said to have sailed to Devon from Wales in a stone coffin! He built a church on the site where he found a sow suckling her piglets, just as a vision had foretold. He won over the locals by teaching them how to till the earth, and used two wild deer to pull his plough. On one occasion a neighbour stole Brannoc's cow, slaughtered it, cut it up and boiled it in a tasty stew. Alerted by the mouth-watering aroma of the simmering bovine, the saint called out the cow's name, whereupon the beast reassembled itself, jumped from the pot, and returned to its rightful owner. When he died, Brannoc was buried inside the church where his likeness is still depicted on a 16th-century bench-end.

ABOVE: A carving in St Brannoc's Church recalls the founding saint's vision that guided him to build a church on the spot where he saw a sow suckling her piglets.

BELOW: The red-tinged waters of Glastonbury's Chalice Well were once thought to have been stained with the blood of Christ, whose uncle, Joseph of Arimathea, is said to have buried the fabled Holy Grail here.

Glastonbury Tor and Abbey
The Mystical Isle of Avalon
GLASTONBURY, SOMERSET

Rising over the marshy Somerset plains, and crowned by the austere tower of St Michael's Chapel, the mysterious dome of Glastonbury Tor is a magical place. Long ago, the surrounding plains were covered by water and the Tor was probably an island, hence its later identification as the mystical Isle of Avalon, to which that 'dusky barge, dark as a funeral scarf from stern to stern' bore the dying King Arthur.

Glastonbury had been designated sacred long before the age of Arthur. Tradition holds that, in the early days of Christianity, St Joseph of Arimathea arrived in England to preach the Gospel, bringing with him the chalice from the Last Supper – the fabled Holy Grail. Climbing the middle one of Glastonbury's three hills (of which the Tor is the highest), and weary from his journey, Joseph rested. He drove his staff into the ground where it took root and flowered, becoming the celebrated Glastonbury Thorn. The bush blossomed every Christmas until it was cut down by a zealous Puritan in the 17th century. Today, the middle hill is known as Wearyall Hill, and a scion of the original thorn grows upon its summit.

Having recovered his strength, Joseph is said to have built a chapel close to where the ruins of Glastonbury Abbey now stand. This was later believed to have been the first Christian site in England, and from its foundations sprang Glastonbury's reputation as one of the holiest places on Earth. As the original chapel flourished into a magnificent monastic foundation

ABOVE: Little now remains of Glastonbury Abbey, once one of England's most magnificent monastic foundations and the place where King Arthur was reputedly buried.

so the legends of Glastonbury grew. In the 6th century, St Collen, who lived as a hermit in a cell atop the tor, was invited to meet with Gwyn ap Nudd, the King of the Fairies, whose palace is said to be underneath the hill. Having declined Gwyn's offer of food, Collen doused him in holy water, whereupon Gwyn and his palace vanished, leaving Collen alone upon the cold hillside.

It is also reputed that Joseph of Arimathea buried the Grail beneath Chalice Hill, the third of Glastonbury's three hills. In the gardens beneath its slopes, ice-cold water, stained red by its high iron content, babbles from an ornate well head. It was once thought to be the blood of Christ that caused the discoloration, and medieval pilgrims would kneel here, trembling and crying.

In 1184 the old abbey was destroyed by fire. Henry II contributed generously to the rebuilding work, and by 1186 the lovely Romanesque Lady Chapel at the west end of the church had been completed. In 1190 the monks, apparently acting on information passed to them by Henry prior to his death in 1189, began making 'strenuous efforts' to find Arthur's grave. Deep beneath the abbey cemetery they found what were purported to be the skeletons of Arthur and Guinevere, with a leaden cross, inscribed in Latin with either, 'Here lies Arthur, the famous King of the Isle of Avalon' or 'Here lies Arthur, king that was, king that shall be.'

It is likely that the 'find' was in fact a 'plant', orchestrated on Henry II's behalf by the monks of Glastonbury. Arthur was a legendary hero of the Britons whose descendents, the Welsh, Henry was attempting to suppress. The Welsh clung doggedly to the belief that Arthur was asleep in a cave somewhere in Wales, and that he would return one day to lead them to victory. The convenient discovery of Arthur's remains buried this notion once and for all. Following Henry's death the monks may simply have put the finishing touches to the revised version of Arthur's legend, and duly uncovered his bones. On 19th April 1278, the two skeletons were re-interred in a black marble tomb inside the church. The tomb, along with much of the abbey, was destroyed at the Dissolution, and a modern plaque is all that now marks its site.

Today Glastonbury is a special and mystical place. No one who has been there early in the morning, when a ghostly mist smothers the surrounding fields, with the domed bulk of Glastonbury Tor rising above, appearing as an island once more, can fail to be moved by its magic.

CADBURY CASTLE
King Arthur's Camelot
SOUTH CADBURY, SOMERSET

ABOVE: A climb to the summit of Cadbury Hill brings the visitor to the most likely site of King Arthur's legendary castle of Camelot, beneath which Arthur may still sleep.

Legends surrounding this tree-shrouded hill, looming over a patchwork landscape of hedgerows and fields, extend far back into the foggy mists of time. Having undertaken the ankle-jarring climb to the lofty heights of what was originally an Iron Age hill fort, you are treated to a breathtaking vista from a truly regal summit that has long held the crown of likeliest contender for King Arthur's Camelot.

The King Arthur of popular imagination is a medieval invention. Those who arrive at Cadbury Castle expecting to find a turreted fortress will be disappointed. Cadbury has never boasted that sort of Norman bastion; it is the fortified hill itself that was the castle. If there was an historical Arthur, he is most likely to have lived in the 5th or 6th centuries, and this is just the sort of hilltop stronghold he would have inhabited.

The first known reference to Cadbury as Camelot is from the antiquarian John Leland who, in 1542, wrote that, 'At the very south end of the church of South-Cadbyri standeth Camallate, sometime a famous town or castle… The people can tell nothing there but that they have heard say Arthur much resorted to Camalat.' Despite claims by sceptics that Leland invented the association, Arthurian lore has surrounded the site ever since. An ancient track that runs from the base of the hill towards Glastonbury has long been known as King Arthur's hunting track, and tradition maintains that Arthur sleeps beyond iron gates hidden in a cave beneath the hill. So ingrained was this legend by the 19th century that, when a group of Victorian archaeologists came to the district, an old man enquired earnestly if they had come to 'dig up the king?'

Interestingly, an archaeological investigation of the 17.3-hectare (18-acre) site in the 1960s revealed that the Iron Age hill fort was massively refortified during the 6th century, when Arthur is believed to have flourished. The undertaking was colossal; whoever ordered it must have been a powerful and significant figure. Of course, it is romantic speculation to suggest that it was King Arthur himself that ordered it. The closest we can come to claiming Cadbury Castle as the site where Britain's most legendary monarch constructed his most mythical castle is to say cautiously 'it might have been'.

Temples to Forgotten Gods: Where Giants Roam the Hills

Alone, alone,
Upon a mossy stone,
She sits and reckons up the dead and gone
With the last leaves for a love-rosary,
Whilst all the wither'd world looks drearily,
Like a dim picture of the drownèd past
In the hush'd mind's mysterious far away,
Doubtful what ghostly thing will steal the last
Into that distance, gray upon the gray.

FROM *AUTUMN*

BY THOMAS HOOD (1798–1845)

DORSET, HAMPSHIRE & WILTSHIRE

Once forming the core of the Saxon kingdom of Wessex, and dominated by the vast chalk lands of Salisbury Plain, this tranquil landscape has the mark of history and legend writ large over its mysterious hillsides and ancient towns. It was here, under the inspired leadership of Alfred the Great, that the English nation was born. It was along its dusty byways, now littered with memories of Arthurian battles, that the Roman legions tramped, pausing to immerse themselves in the hot natural waters at the place we today call Bath, the founding of which legend attributes to Bladud, father of King Lear. Long before any of this, however, a forgotten and mysterious people had cast their shadow across the landscape. They carved strange figures onto the chalk hillsides, and erected massive earthworks, which later generations would come to believe could only have been effected by the Devil. Most impressive of all were the two immense stone temples at Avebury and Stonehenge, which still amaze and confound us today some 3,000 to 4,000 years later.

KEY

1. The Cerne Abbas Giant
2. Badbury Rings
3. St Olave's Church
4. Winchester
5. Wherwell Priory
6. Old Sarum
7. Silbury Hill
8. The Roman Baths

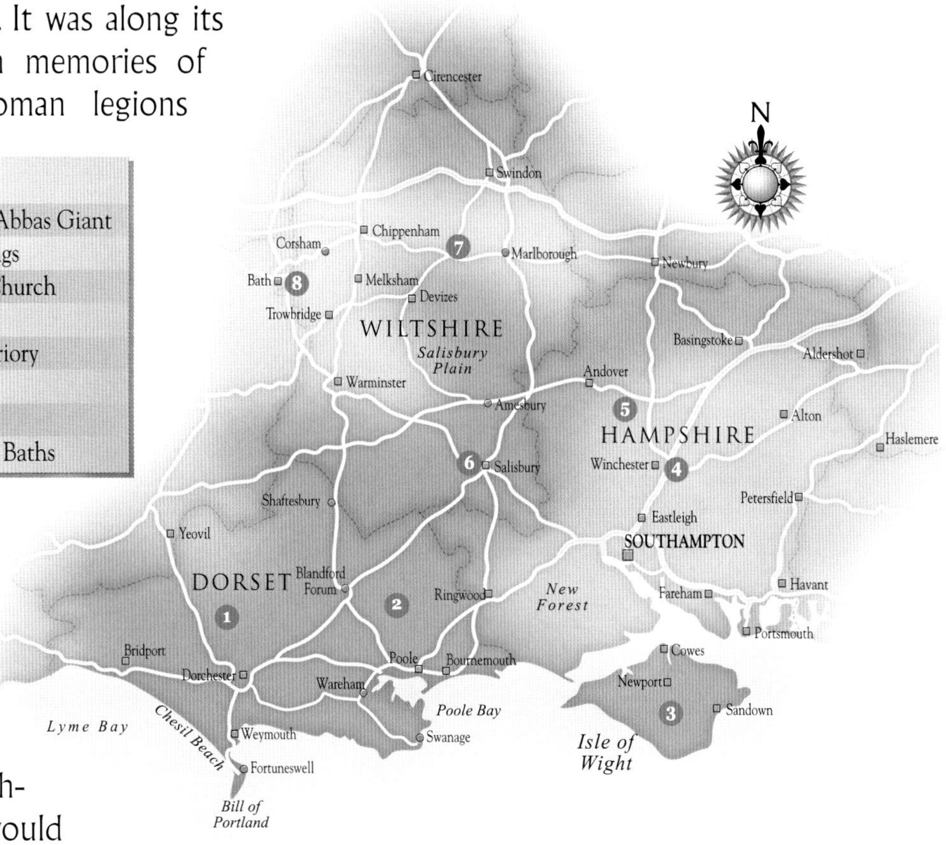

THE CERNE ABBAS GIANT
The Invading Giant
CERNE ABBAS, DORSET

Standing an impressive 55 metres (180 feet) tall, the club-wielding Cerne Abbas Giant is the most detailed of all Britain's hill figures, resplendent with eyes, nose, mouth, breasts, ribs – and genitalia of such awesome proportions that they can only be truly appreciated from the air. Indeed, he has long been regarded as a fertility symbol whose assistance has been eagerly sought by courting and married couples alike, many of whom (it is rumoured) have consummated their relationships between his massive chalk thighs.

His origins, however, are lost in a swirling haze of folklore and speculation. Several historians believe that he depicts the Greek-Roman god Hercules and that he was carved during the reign of Emperor Commodus (AD180–93) who, believing himself to be a reincarnation of Hercules, revived his cult. Legend, on the other hand, asserts that the figure represents an invading giant who fell asleep on the hillside and was decapitated by the local people, who carved his outline into the chalk as a warning to other marauders. A third hypothesis points to the fact that his 9-metre (30-foot) phallus is directly aligned to the rising sun on 1st May and this, coupled with the fact that May Day celebrations were once held on the hill above the giant's head, seems to suggest that he may have been linked to an ancient fertility ritual.

Whatever his origins, his presence has long been a source of amusement and controversy. Perhaps the last word should go to local dignitary, the Hon. Ophelia Pashley-Cumming, who once observed, 'I have never felt affronted by the Cerne Giant, and have no time for the simpering old ladies who cluck-cluck every time they pass it. The only residents I sympathize with are the elderly males or tired Dorchester businessmen who are constantly reminded by their wives and mistresses en passant of how far short they fall of the splendid male vigour displayed before them.

BADBURY RINGS
Arthur's Greatest Victory
NR WIMBORNE MINSTER, DORSET

This stunning Iron Age hill fort, overlooking the tranquil Dorset countryside, has a long, eventful history and a near mythical status as a possible contender for the site of the Battle of Badon Hill, at which King Arthur won his decisive victory over the Saxons.

According to Geoffrey of Monmouth, Arthur had already defeated the Saxons in the north and the vanquished enemy had

PREVIOUS PAGES: Legend claims that Merlin oversaw the transportation of Stonehenge's colossal stones from Wales to Salisbury Plain, where they still stand today.

ABOVE: The origins of the Cerne Abbas Giant may be lost in a mist of debate and speculation, but he still inspires wonder, and postcards of him are said to be the only overtly pornographic images that the local post office will carry!

pledged to return to their own land. Having set sail, however, they broke their promise and headed south round the coast to land at Torbay. From here they headed inland and, having indulged in a fair amount of pillage, arrived on the summit of

ABOVE: The wood-bound heights of Badbury Rings are where King Arthur is said to have won a decisive victory over his Saxon adversaries at the Battle of Badon Hill.

Mount Badon where they made their camp. Arthur hurried south and, despite the Saxons holding an advantageous position, rallied his men to attempt a brave assault. Raising his mighty sword, Excalibur, Arthur charged up the hill and killed 470 Saxons. Emboldened by his superhuman example, his followers stormed after him and routed the enemy once and for all.

ST OLAVE'S CHURCH
The Legend of Lucy Lightfoot
GATCOMBE, ISLE OF WIGHT

Gatcombe's village church was built in 1292 for the Estur family, one of whom, Edward, is commemorated by a splendid oak carving of a crusading knight that can be seen inside. Around the wooden carving a delightful tale of mysterious intrigue has been woven.

In the early 19th century, Lucy Lightfoot, a farmer's daughter from the nearby village of Bowcombe, used to spend hours gazing at this effigy. When asked why, she is said to have replied, 'I love to be with him on his adventures.' On the morning of 13th June 1831, a ferocious thunderstorm shook the district, coinciding with a total eclipse of the sun. When the tempest had abated, a farmer noticed Lucy's horse tethered to the church gates, and went inside to check on her. He found that the building was empty, and despite several searches she was never seen again.

In 1865 the Reverend Samuel Trelawney was researching the history of the Crusades when he chanced upon a document that added a bizarre twist to Lucy's disappearance. The manuscript, written by the Chancellor to the King of Cyprus in 1365, mentioned a group of knights who that year left London to fight in the Crusades. One of them, Edward Estur, was accompanied by his mistress — a 'brave woman' from the Isle of Wight — whose name was Lucy Lightfoot. When they arrived in Cyprus, the two lovers bade each other farewell and Edward headed for Alexandria, where he was seriously injured in battle and, due to the effects of a head wound, forgot all about his mistress.

Numerous fanciful theories have been put forward to explain this tantalizing enigma, with many paranormal investigators wondering if the 19th-century Lucy Lightfoot was the victim of a time slip that reunited her with her former self in a sort of 'pre' incarnation. In fact, the whole saga serves as an example of how legends develop, for her story is actually a late 20th-century work of fiction by James Evans, former rector of the parish. What the vicar intended as a light-hearted yarn, that might possibly raise a few pennies for church coffers, has travelled far beyond the sylvan boundaries of the churchyard and found its way into numerous books and magazine articles, where it is presented as historical fact. 'Little did I think,' wrote James Evans to Mark Wightman, whose investigations unveiled the truth behind the mystery, 'that I had given her [Lucy Lightfoot] invisible wings to fly to many places and to speed down the years.'

ABOVE: The mystery of Lucy Lightfoot has drawn investigators of the paranormal from far and wide to St Olave's Church, despite being a fiction of the late 20th century!

BELOW: Preoccupied with thoughts of winning back his kingdom from the Danes, King Alfred fails to notice that the cakes are burning in the herdsman's cottage.

WINCHESTER
St Swithun, King Alfred and the Round Table
WINCHESTER, HAMPSHIRE

Few towns have enjoyed greater historical importance than Winchester, which was for centuries the capital of the Saxon and Norman Kings of England. Today, it is a peaceful cathedral city, steeped in history, rich in architecture and dominated by its great grey cathedral, to the left of which are the foundations of the Saxon foundation, where St Swithun was buried in AD861. According to legend, this pious and saintly man asked to be laid to rest in the open, where men might trample over his bones and the rains of heaven fall upon him. When his body was later moved inside the cathedral, the skies opened and it rained in torrents for just over six weeks. From this apocryphal story comes the tradition that, if it rains on St Swithun's Day (15th July), it will continue to do so for 40 days.

Dominating one of the city's main thoroughfares — Broadway — is an

impressive statue of Alfred the Great (849–900), who was crowned at Winchester in 871. It was he who drove the Danes from southern England, and it is he whom history remembers as being the founder of a unified English nation. A famous legend about Alfred dates from the tempestuous years of his early reign, when he was struggling to repel the Viking threat. On Twelfth Night 878, the Danish leader Guthrum launched a surprise attack on Alfred's stronghold at Chippenham. The king narrowly escaped and, with a small band of followers, fled to the swamps of Somerset's Isle of Athelney. He took shelter in a herdsman's cottage. The herdsman's wife asked her visitor to watch her cakes. Preoccupied with his troubles, Alfred let them burn. When the woman returned she was furious, and was, of course, unaware of Alfred's identity. She subjected him to a severe tongue-lashing. 'Can't ye mind the cakes, man, and didn't ye see them burning?' she harangued him,

ABOVE: The 14th-century Round Table in Winchester may not have been used by King Arthur, but Henry VIII showed it off to the visiting French emperor Charles V.

BELOW: The fearsome cockatrice, like the one that terroized the Wherwell neighbourhood in the Middle Ages, was a deadly combination of fowl and dragon.

'I'm bound ye eats them fast enough.' By the spring of 878, Alfred was able to put culinary disasters and regal setbacks behind him. Rallying his forces, he launched his counter-offensive and won back his kingdom.

There is also a tradition that Winchester was the site of Camelot, and in the Great Hall can be seen what is purported to be King Arthur's Round Table. Although it most certainly is not, it is a splendid piece of carpentry, measuring 5.5 metres (18 feet) across and weighing over a ton. It hangs on the hall's west wall and may have done so since the 14th century. Henry VIII later had the figure of King Arthur painted on it (originally in the likeness of Henry himself), added a Tudor rose to the centre and the names of 24 knights around the rim. In 1522, he brought the French Emperor Charles V to see it in order to demonstrate the antiquity of the English throne and, more importantly, Henry's right to sit upon it.

'CAN'T YE MIND THE CAKES, MAN, AND DIDN'T YE SEE THEM BURNING? I'M BOUND YE EATS THEM FAST ENoUGH.'

THE HERDSMAN'S WIFE TO KING ALFRED

WHERWELL PRIORY
The Wherwell Cockatrice
WHERWELL, NR ANDOVER, HAMPSHIRE

In 1538 a toad is said to have incubated a cock's egg in the cellars of Wherwell Priory. When it hatched, a fearful, winged creature emerged that the nuns instantly recognized as a cock-atrice. This legendary beast of the Middle Ages was imagined as having the head of a cockerel, the wings of a fowl and the tail of a dragon. Such was the power of its gaze that it could kill people simply by looking at them.

True to its dreadful reputation, the serpent was soon despatching people all over the district, and a reward of 1.6 hectares (4 acres) of land was offered to anyone who could kill it. Many tried, but all died in the attempt. A servant by the name of Green, however, had a flash of inspiration. He lowered a sheet of burnished metal into the lair of the cockatrice. Seeing its own reflection, the creature lashed out in an attempt to kill the intruder and continued to do so for several days before falling exhausted to the ground. Green promptly leapt into its den and finished it off with a spear.

Old Sarum
Old Sarum's Fall from Grace
NR SALISBURY, WILTSHIRE

First settled in the Bronze Age, Old Sarum was later occupied by the Romans, Saxons, Danes and finally the Normans. It became a bishopric in 1075 and the saintly bishop, Osmund, began its cathedral. His successor, Bishop Roger, was a different type of churchman. His rise to eminence began when Henry I stopped to hear mass at the church where Roger was officiating and, delighted by the speed of the service, made him royal chaplain. Such were Roger's administrative skills that he was soon appointed chancellor and awarded the bishopric at Sarum. As one of the richest and most powerful men in the country, he rebuilt the cathedral of Sarum, refortified the castle and awarded influential positions to his mistress and their son. After Henry's death, however, officers of the new king, Stephen, arrested Roger, charged him with treason and stripped him of power and wealth. He died shortly afterwards of a broken heart.

With Bishop Roger's fall from favour, Old Sarum went into decline, and constant friction arose between the civil and religious authorities. This, coupled with the disadvantages of the site (including a shortage of water), made the dean and chapter decide to petition for their cathedral to be removed to the plain below. The building, they complained, was exposed to continuous gusts of wind that were so noisy it was impossible for the clerks to hear one another sing. Furthermore, the site's lack of trees and grass meant that the chalk on which it stood gave off such a glare that many of the clergy had gone blind. 'Let us in God's name,' they pleaded, 'descend into the plain.' Their prayers were answered and in 1220, under the leadership of Bishop Poore, the clergy began the removal. Legend says that an archer was asked to shoot an arrow from the heights of Old Sarum and, where it fell, Salisbury Cathedral was built.

Where the clergy led, the townsfolk followed, and soon Old Sarum was little more than a ghost town. Bramble, bracken, nettle and ivy crept over its walls and sprang through its pathways as nature reclaimed the hilltop. Today an aura of indefinable mystery, amplified by the serenity of the surrounding countryside, emanates from Old Sarum's earthen mounds and rain-washed stones and you get the distinct impression that the eyes of bygone residents are following your every step.

BELOW: The Bronze Age site of Old Sarum is now a ghost town of crumbling walls, ancient pathways and earthen mounds, along with memories of its former glories.

SILBURY HILL
Europe's Largest Man-made Mound
NR MARLBOROUGH, WILTSHIRE

This awe-inspiring wonder, dating from around 2700BC, is almost 40 metres (130 feet) high, and covers 2.25 hectares (5.5 acres). It has been estimated that it would have taken 700 men 10 years of continuous labour to fashion the 12 million cubic feet of earth, chalk and stone into the breathtaking monument that confronts us today. Yet no one knows why it was built or even what purpose it originally served.

Numerous scientific and archaeological theories have been put forward. Local legend, meanwhile, maintains that the Devil was once on his way to dump a huge sack of earth onto the citizens of Marlborough, when the Druid priests at nearby Avebury used their magic to stop him. The Devil emptied the earth from his sack and thus created Silbury Hill. Another tradition claims that the hill is the grave of a king whose name was Sil. He sits at the centre of the mound, wearing a golden suit of armour, astride a gold-clad horse. With the possibility of such potential riches lying within, Silbury Hill has been subjected to numerous excavations, but nothing of note has ever been found and it remains a silent testimony to a forgotten people at whose skills and beliefs we can only marvel.

THE ROMAN BATHS
Prince Bladud
BATH, AVON

The 22.5 million litres (half-a-million gallons) of thermal mineral water that gush from the ground every day at around 48°C (118.4°F) have drawn tourists to Bath for 2,000 years. The Romans founded the city when they encountered here a spring dedicated to the Celtic goddess of healing, Sul. Identifying her with their own deity, Minerva, they built a temple dedicated to Sul Minerva, and named the town that grew up around it Aqae Sulis or 'Sul's Spa'. It was soon famous for its curative waters, and the structures built to house the spring were some of the finest in Roman Britain. The city we see today, however, is largely an 18th-century creation, by which time Bath had acquired a legendary founder, Prince Bladud.

As a youth, Bladud contracted leprosy and his parents banished him from the Royal Court. He became a swineherd on the banks of the Avon opposite the future site of Bath. One day, to his horror, he discovered that the pigs had caught his disease and herded them across the river, whilst he considered how to break the news to their owner. No sooner had they arrived on the opposite bank than the pigs raced off and plunged into a nearby hot spring where, despite Bladud's best efforts, they refused to leave. Eventually he managed to coax them out by laying a trail of acorns, and when Bladud wiped away the mud he found that their leprosy was gone. Racing back to the pool he threw himself in and was also cured.

Returning to his father's court, he assumed his rightful position and, when he became king, founded the city of Bath at the site of his cure. Legend holds that he became a great patron of learning. He was also a dabbler in the magical arts, and having made himself a pair of wings was out flying one day when suddenly he fell to earth and was killed, leaving his son Lear to succeed him as king.

ABOVE: Local legend says that a king named Sil, clad in golden armour, sits upon his gold-clad mount at the heart of Silbury Hill.

OPPOSITE: Although the Romans actually founded the city of Bath, legend claims it as the work of Prince Bladud, father of the more famous King Lear.

Royal Mistresses, Holy Hermits and Ancient Kings

Over hill, over dale,
Thorough bush, thorough brier,
Over park, over pale,
Thorough flood, thorough fire,
I do wander everywhere,
Swifter than the moon's sphere;
And I serve the fairy queen,
To dew her orbs upon the green.
The cowslips tall her pensioners be:
In their gold coats spots you see;
Those be rubies, fairy favours,
In those freckles live their savours:
I must go seek some dewdrops here
And hang a pearl in every cowslip's ear.

FROM *A MIDSUMMER NIGHT'S DREAM*
BY WILLIAM SHAKESPEARE (1564–1616)

GLOUCESTERSHIRE, HEREFORD-SHIRE, WORCESTERSHIRE, WARWICKSHIRE & OXFORDSHIRE

T he counties that stretch westwards from Oxfordshire to Herefordshire offer the intrepid seeker after Britain's ancient mysteries a veritable cornucopia of history, myth and legend. It is a tranquil region of fertile valleys and sky-swept hills, steeped in contradictions. Wandering the quiet Warwickshire highways and byways along which Shakespeare once traipsed, or meandering amongst the gentle hills of the Cotswolds, it is almost impossible to believe that this is a battle-scarred landscape where so many momentous events of national importance have taken place that it has long been known as 'England's cockpit'. It was here that Charles I established his headquarters in the dark days of the Civil War. The Saxons drove the native Britons through here towards the brooding, rugged mountains beyond the border with Wales, and began a struggle for mastery of southern England that would last for almost 600 years. Here, an ancient people stamped their imprint upon the countryside, leaving behind them mysterious hill figures, burial chambers and imposing fortresses. All in all it is a landscape that can fire the imagination and yet soothe the spirits of even the most jaded 21st-century city dweller.

KEY

1. All Saints Church
2. Winchcombe
3. Chipping Campden Hall
4. St Dubricius Church
5. The Church of St Mary and St David
6. Worcester Cathedral
7. Charlecote Park
8. Rosamund's Well, Blenheim Palace
9. Wayland's Smithy

ALL SAINTS CHURCH
The Bonehouse and the Bisley Boy
BISLEY, GLOUCESTERSHIRE

The magnificent spire of Bisley Church is visible from miles around. In the churchyard there is a 12th-century well head that commemorates a long ago tragedy. One night the parish priest was summoned to administer the last rites to a dying parishioner. When he failed to arrive, a search was launched and his body was found at the bottom of the well. He had evidently lost his way in the dark and plunged to his death. To avert such a tragedy happening again, a cover was constructed over the deep drop.

In the 19th century, workmen excavating the site for a new school, adjacent to nearby Over Court, found a medieval stone coffin containing the bones of a young girl. They were, without doubt, those of a forgotten daughter of the village. The vicar, Thomas Keble, used the find to create one of the region's more colourful legends. As a girl, Queen Elizabeth I had once stayed at Over Court and, according to Keble, had died during her visit. Fearing the wrath of Henry VIII, the frightened villagers put a child of the same age in her place, and so covered up the tragedy. The nearest likeness they could find, however, was a young boy, whom they dressed in Elizabeth's clothes and sent back to the royal court. When the 'Bisley Boy' grew up and became monarch of England, he could never marry for fear of revealing the deception, which is why he reigned from 1558 to 1603 as 'the Virgin Queen'.

WINCHCOMBE
The Legend of St Kenelm
WINCHCOMBE, GLOUCESTERSHIRE

In Saxon times, Winchcombe was the capital of Winchcombshire in the Kingdom of Mercia. It was here in AD798 that King Kenulf founded a monastery, which, by the time of his death in AD821, had blossomed into one of the most prosperous foundations in England. His seven-year-old son, Kenelm, inherited the throne and was placed under the guardianship of his elder sister, Quendreda. This evil woman harboured personal ambitions and so set about scheming and plotting her brother's assassination.

She persuaded her brother's tutor, Askobert, to murder Kenelm, and he took the boy hunting in the forest of Clent. As they entered the woodland, Askobert suddenly turned on

ABOVE: Known locally as 'the Bone Chute' because remnants of parishioners were once placed there, Bisley's well cover was meant to protect people from falling into it.

PREVIOUS PAGES: The grounds of Chipping Campden Hall, where a mysterious disappearance resulted in one of the Cotswolds' most intriguing legends.

his young charge and sliced off his head with his sword. As the wicked tutor was burying the corpse, a white dove flew from the disembodied skull. It encircled the murder site, then disappeared. Askobert finished his task and reported back to Quendedra. Delighted, she settled down to enjoy the fruits of her infamy, but not for long. The dove flew to Rome where it dropped a parchment detailing the heinous crime, at the feet of the Pope. Envoys were dispatched to England and, following a search, the tiny corpse was discovered and borne back to Winchcombe. The evil Quendreda saw the mournful procession and, realizing that her crime had been discovered, attempted to curse the cortège by reciting Psalm 109 backwards. Instantly her eyes exploded from their sockets and her blood spattered the pages of the psalter from which she was reading.

Kenelm was laid to rest alongside his father and a shrine was erected over his body. It became an important place of pilgrimage and continued so until its dissolution in the 16th century, after which it fell into ruin. In 1815, excavations uncovered two stone caskets containing the remains of a man and a child and, although the bones are said to have disintegrated on contact with the air, the coffins can still be seen inside the parish church.

ABOVE: The caskets that may once have contained the bones of King Kenulf and his saintly son St Kenelm are kept inside Winchcombe's church.

CHIPPING CAMPDEN HALL
The Campden Wonder
CHIPPING CAMPDEN, GLOUCESTERSHIRE

Chipping Campden's old hall was built in 1613 by Sir Baptist Hicks, the first Viscount Campden and was by all accounts, a splendidly opulent Jacobean mansion. It lasted just 30 years before being burnt down by Royalist troops who had garrisoned it during the Civil War.

Following the house's destruction, William Harrison became administrator of the manorial lands round about on behalf of Lady Campden. On Thursday 16th August, 1660, 70-year-old Harrison set out to collect rents in the nearby hamlet of Charringworth. When he hadn't come back by dusk, his wife sent their servant, John Perry, to look for him; he also failed to return. The following morning the couple's son, Edward, set out to enquire after his father, and met Perry on the road to Charringworth. On the way back to Chipping Campden, the son and the servant met an old woman who showed them a mangled hat and bloody collar band, which

she had found in a nearby field. Edward immediately recognized the items as his father's, but although a thorough search was undertaken, no trace of the missing steward was found.

Harrison's family immediately began to suspect that John Perry was somehow involved in his master's disappearance. When brought before the local magistrate, he confessed that he and his brother, Richard, had waylaid Harrison near Chipping Campden churchyard. Richard had murdered Harrison and then disposed of the body, aided by their mother, Joan. Richard and Joan were arrested and, despite protesting their innocence and there being no tangible evidence against them, they were charged and sent for trial, along with John.

The three were tried at Gloucester assizes where they were found guilty of murder and sentenced to death. Their execution took place on Broadway Hill, a little way outside Chipping Campden. Joan Perry was the first to die. It was commonly believed that she was a witch, and that she was using her powers to prevent Richard from confessing. When Richard mounted the scaffold, he professed his innocence and implored his brother to tell the truth. John steadfastly refused and watched as his brother was hanged. Finally, the noose was placed around John's neck and, with his dying breath, he confessed that he knew nothing whatsoever about William Harrison's fate. The townsfolk returned home, no doubt relieved at having rid themselves of an unpleasant and murderous family.

Two years later, who should come strolling into town but William Harrison! He told the local magistrate, Sir Thomas Overbury, that three mysterious horsemen had abducted him and sold him to slave traders. Eventually he became the property of an elderly physician in the Turkish town of Smyrna, where he worked in his master's distillery and was given a silver bowl to drink from. After nearly two years there the physician died and Harrison escaped to a nearby port, where he used the silver bowl to bribe his way onto a ship bound for Lisbon. From there he worked his passage to Dover and then walked to Chipping Campden. Since William Harrison's account is too far-fetched to be believable, many solutions have been put forward to explain what became known as the 'Campden Wonder'. One theory holds that Harrison may have believed that Joan Perry had bewitched him, and his disappearance was an elaborate ruse aimed at freeing himself from her baleful influence. It has also been suggested that Harrison may have been a spy who was sent abroad on some top-secret mission.

Whatever the reason for his absence, it seems that he had not anticipated the confession of John Perry, whose motives are destined to remain one of the greatest conundrums of a riveting mystery.

St Dubricius Church
The Man who Crowned Arthur
HENTLAND, HEREFORDSHIRE

Saint Dubricius flourished during the first half of the 6th century during that enigmatic period of history known as 'the Dark Ages'. From the few records we have of him, he appears to have been an extremely prolific abbot or bishop who trained over 2,000 priests at his monastery, which stood near to the 14th-century church that now bears his name. Fable, however, remembers him as one of the most powerful churchmen of his age, and has bestowed upon him a reputation of such posthumous importance that even his origins are considered supernatural.

Dubricius was the son of Princess Eurddil. Her father, Peibau, King of Archenfield, was known as 'King Dribbler' thanks to his uncontrollable habit of foaming at the mouth. One day, the king found that his unmarried daughter was pregnant and ordered his courtiers to drown her in the River Wye as punishment. However, when they tied the princess into a sack and cast her into the raging waters, the current simply washed her, unharmed, back to the shore. Three times they tried to carry out the king's sentence,

ABOVE: Chipping Campden churchyard, which a servant falsely claimed, was the site where his mother and brother had murdered his master.

but each time the river delivered her safely back to land. So the king ruled that she was to be burnt alive, and she was flung onto a blazing pyre. Next morning, messengers came to retrieve her bones and found her sitting unharmed amongst the ashes, the infant Dubricius on her lap. Mother and child were promptly taken before the king who, realizing the injustice of his ways, welcomed them with open arms. His grandson reached out and touched his face, and he never foamed at the mouth again. It is now impossible to

ABOVE: The hidden-away church in Hentland dedicated to St Dubricius commemorates a Dark Age cleric whom legend says crowned King Arthur.

RIGHT: Kilpeck's Sheela-Na-Gig – a female figure exposing her genitalia – is just one of over 100 such symbols that appear on churches all over Britain.

OPPOSITE: A rich array of pagan symbols adorns the doorway of the Church of St Mary and St David at Kilpeck.

separate fact from fiction in the colourful life of this tantalizing cleric. A contemporary description of Dubricius as being 'a candle on a stand' is probably the closest we will come to understanding the inspirational effect he had on his fellow Britons. At the time, people were wracked by political uncertainties and under constant attack from Germanic and Gaelic invaders, and may well have looked to him for guidance and some reassurance. Indeed, such was his mythical status that later generations came to believe that he could have been the only cleric capable of crowning the legendary King Arthur.

THE CHURCH OF ST MARY AND ST DAVID
Sheela-Na-Gig
KILPECK, HEREFORDSHIRE

Kilpeck Church is a peaceful little building dating from the 12th century. Its crowning glory is its south doorway, around which a stunning array of pagan and Christian motifs bear testimony to the humour and skills of the craftsmen, who created them almost 1,000 years ago. The most controversial and enigmatic of them is the Sheela-Na-Gig.

'Sheela-Na-Gig' is a collective name, used to describe over 100 such carvings found predominantly on churches – but also on other important buildings – all over England and Ireland. They depict naked females, posed in a manner that displays and emphasizes their genitalia. The name is of Irish origin, and possibly derived from a common Gaelic expression meaning an immodest woman. She has been variously described as a device to ward off evil spirits; a sexual stimulant; an obscene old hag; a fertility symbol; or a depiction of the Mother Goddess.

There is a common consensus that the Sheela-Na-Gig was a Christian invention, which incorporated Celtic symbolism; the almost triangular head and the huge round eyes are reminiscent of early Celtic art. It has been suggested that the medieval church may have allowed a powerful pre-Christian figure to coexist with its own imagery, or even that it adopted this exhibitionist female as a means of warning against the sins of the flesh. Another widely held belief, particularly in Ireland, maintains that she is a fertility symbol. Yet, although her wide-open legs and exaggerated vulva imply fertility, the upper half of the figure is either shown as being childishly flat-chested, or having long drooping breasts that suggest extreme old age. In other words, she could be seen as a symbol of fertility *and* infertility.

Also included amongst the many carvings in the church is the figure of that enigmatic old folk symbol, the so-called 'Green Man'. These well-known and ebullient figures which depict human heads surrounded by a profusion of leaves, are

found on churches all over Britain, the generic term 'Green Man' was actually invented in 1939 by Lady Raglan, who first used it in an article in *Folk-Lore*. The reason why so many medieval stonemasons should choose to carve these possibly pagan symbols onto ecclesiastical buildings is unknown. One suggestion is that the Green Man was a depiction of the spirit or god of the yearly renewal of life. To an essentially agricultural country such as Britain this would have been vitally important. The Christian Church may have simply adopted the symbol as a representation of mortal life – birth, life, death decay – all of which the soul could overcome with faith, thus allowing Christianity and pagan folk beliefs to sit comfortably side by side.

The truth is that we will never know for sure why bygone craftsmen chose to adorn so many sacred buildings with overtly pagan and seemingly obscene imagery. Perhaps our desire to believe in ancient symbolism has blinded us to what may have been nothing more than a bawdy joke, carved for the amusement of his workmates by a long-forgotten craftsman.

ABOVE: The effigy on King John's tomb in Worcester Cathedral may well be the oldest royal example in England.

WORCESTER CATHEDRAL
The Tomb of King John
WORCESTER, WORCESTERSHIRE

King John (1167–1216), the fourth and youngest son of Henry II, was the archetypal wicked king, whose record of rebellion and intrigue against his brother, Richard I, led contemporary historian William of Newburgh (1135–98) to denounce him as 'nature's enemy'. The king's bullying manner and excessive taxation provoked the powerful English barons to rebel against him, and force him to seal the Magna Carta. Later hailed as a declaration of English liberties, the charter was at the time little more than a criticism of John's style of government. He had no intention of adhering to its terms. His reign ended with England wracked by civil war.

One place he had reverence for was Worcester and, as he lay dying, he made a codicil to his will ordering that he was to be buried in its cathedral, between the tombs of its two saints, St Oswald and St Wulfstan. Their bones were dispersed long ago, but the tomb of 'evil' King John still exists. Its marble top is the lid of his original coffin, and it is thought to be the oldest royal effigy in England.

The tomb has been opened several times, shedding light upon a legend concerning the king's final days. It is said that John, realizing that his chances of attaining heaven were limited, gave orders that his corpse was to be dressed in the garb of a monk. Thus attired, he hoped to hoodwink his way into Paradise. When the tomb was opened in 1797, the remnants of an ancient cowl were supposedly found wrapped around his skull!

CHARLECOTE PARK
Shakespeare the Deerhunter
CHARLECOTE, WARWICKSHIRE

One of the many mysteries concerning William Shakespeare – apart from whether or not he actually wrote the plays attributed to him – is what led him to abandon his family and seek employment in the precarious world of the London theatre? History is mute on the subject, and thus legend and gossip have stepped nimbly into the breach to create a plethora of fanciful theories. One of the most colourful and enduring of these has become indelibly linked with the extensive grounds of Charlecote Park in Warwickshire, and its then owner Sir Thomas Lucy.

Completed in 1558, Charlecote was the first great Elizabethan manor house to be built in Warwickshire. Part of the walled estate was left as a free warren, in the dense undergrowth of which rabbits, hares, foxes, pheasants and other beasts of chase were watched over by several gamekeepers. Whether deer were grazed on the estate in Shakespeare's youth is doubtful, but, according to an 18th-century tradition, he was caught poaching Sir Thomas Lucy's venison, and the enraged landowner punished the transgression with a vicious flogging. The youthful bard, already showing literary

promise, retaliated by libellously lampooning his persecutor in a satirical verse, which he nailed to the entrance gates of Charlecote Park. With the threat of another beating on the horizon, he departed Stratford and fled to London – and the rest, as they say, is history.

ROSAMUND'S WELL, BLENHEIM PALACE
The Fair Rosamund
WOODSTOCK, OXFORDSHIRE

Rosamund was the daughter of Walter de Clifford. She was sent to Godstow Priory, near Oxford, to complete her education, where, legend holds, she caught the eye of Henry II. The king made her his mistress and built her a 'bower' or dwelling in the grounds of his palace at Woodstock (now the spacious park of Blenheim Palace). Around the bower he constructed a complicated maze to protect Rosamund from the prying eyes of his queen, the formidable Eleanor of Aquitaine. One day, having enjoyed an illicit rendezvous with his mistress, the king stepped from the maze to find his wife. She had noticed a length of silk thread snagged upon Henry's spur and had followed its course to the centre of the maze, where she came face-to-face with her husband's lover. She offered Rosamund

ABOVE: Did the fact that Shakespeare was caught poaching deer in Charlecote Park lead to him leaving Stratford for London to avoid punishment?

BELOW: In the grounds of Blenheim Palace are the ragged remnants of Rosamund's Well, built by Henry II for his 'rose of the world', the Fair Rosamund.

the choice of death by sword or death by poison. Rosamund chose the latter and, having imbibed the fatal draught, was buried at Godstow Priory.

In fact, Rosamund appears to have retired by her own volition to Godstow nunnery, where, following her death in 1176, Henry is reputed to have paid generously for the nuns to say prayers for the salvation of her soul. When Bishop Hugh of Lincoln visited Godstow in 1191, he was appalled by the extravagance of her tomb and ordered it to be destroyed. Her bones were reinterred in the chapter house where her new and rather unflattering epitaph is said to have read, 'Here lieth in tomb the rose of the world, not a clean rose; it smelleth not sweet, but it stinketh, that was wont to smell full sweet'!

WAYLAND'S SMITHY
The Magical Smith
NR ASHBURY, OXFORDSHIRE

As you wander along the ancient track known as 'the Ridgeway', you pass by a solemn circle of ageing trees surrounding a mysterious mound. The mound's origins stretch back over 5,000 years to when prehistoric man erected a burial chamber on this windswept crest. Around 3300BC, others arrived, evicted the earlier residents and eclipsed their tomb with a larger, more imposing, earthwork. Another 4,000 years later, Saxon settlers stumbled upon the ancient

'HERE LIETH IN TOMB THE ROSE OF THE WORLD, NOT A CLEAN ROSE; IT SMELLETH NOT SWEET, BUT IT STINKETH, THAT WAS WONT TO SMELL FULL SWEET.'

EPITAPH ON THE TOMB OF ROSAMUND

DE CLIFFORD

OPPOSITE ABOVE: Weland working in his smithy. He was a Saxon adaptation of the Norse Smith *Volundr* whose capture by King Nidudr had terrible repercussions.

ABOVE: The prehistoric burial mound of Wayland's Smithy is a place of Saxon legends.

relic and, utterly mystified as to its origins, attributed it to their god, Weland the Smith.

Weland, or Wayland as he became known, is thought to be the Saxon adaptation of the Norse *Volundr*, a magical smith of such outstanding skill that King Nidudr captured him and, having lamed him to prevent his escape, set him to work at the royal forge. Volundr exacted a dreadful revenge upon his tormentor. First, he lured the king's two sons to the forge and, having murdered them, fashioned their skulls into drinking vessels, which he sent to their father. Next, when the king's daughter asked him to mend a ring, he drugged and raped her. Then, using

his magical powers, he escaped by flying through the air, pausing to taunt the anguished monarch as he passed overhead.

The association of the hillside tomb with the god Weland was certainly established by the 9th century, since a Berkshire charter dated AD855 refers to it as 'Welandes Smidde'. Over succeeding centuries, his fearsome reputation gave way to a gentler, more constructive, persona, and thus by 1738 the antiquarian Francis Wise recorded the tradition:

> At this place lived formerly an invisible Smith, and if a traveller's horse had lost a Shoe upon the road, he had no more to do than to bring the Horse to this place with a piece of money, and leaving both there for some little time, he might come again and find the money gone, but the Horse new shod.

As recently as the 19th century, children would visit Wayland's Smithy and listen for the ghostly pounding of his hammer.

Capital secrets: *Hellish* Aristocrats *and* Ladies of the Road

These, in the day when heaven was falling,
The hour when earth's foundations fled,
Followed their mercenary calling
And took their wages and are dead.

Their shoulders held the sky suspended;
They stood, and earth's foundations stay;
What God abandoned, these defended,
And saved the sum of things for pay.

EPITAPH ON AN ARMY OF MERCENARIES
BY ALFRED EDWARD HOUSMAN (1859–1936)

BUCKINGHAMSHIRE, BERKSHIRE, LONDON, HERTFORDSHIRE & BEDFORDSHIRE

L ondon is steeped in legend and is associated with a great number of famous figures from the past. The city has long been a magnet to ambitious youths who, like Dick Whittington, have come in search of its mythical gold-paved streets. It has also attracted the dishonest and the infamous, such as Dick Turpin and Jack the Ripper, whose legends have become an integral part of the capital's rich folklore. To the north and west of London stretch the counties of Hertfordshire, Bedfordshire, Berkshire and Buckinghamshire, all of which possess rich veins of legend. Satan and his devilish cohorts appear to have been particularly active here; but, on the other hand, religious fervour has been strong, and the likes of John Bunyan are indelibly linked with the area. Add to all this the nefarious activities of the notorious Hell Fire Club and you have a rich and varied mix of legend and lore that sits comfortably amidst a tranquil, and sometimes mysterious, landscape.

KEY

1. St Lawrence Church and the Dashwood Mausoleum
2. Windsor Great Park
3. St Mary le Bow
4. The East End
5. London Bridge
6. The Spaniard's Inn
7. Markyate Cell
8. Holy Trinity Church
9. The Abbey Church of St Mary and St Helena

PREVIOUS PAGES: John Bunyan used to call at Houghton Hall when he earned his living as a tinker. Later he would remember it in *The Pilgrim's Progress*.

LEFT: Charles Dickens called St Olave's, Hart Street, 'The church of St Ghastly Grim because of the skulls that surmount its gateway.' It is dedicated to the Norse King Olaf whose achievement is commemorated in the rhyme 'London Bridge is Falling Down.'

OPPOSITE: The strange golden ball atop St Lawrence Church is just one of the eccentric follies with which Sir Francis Dashwood decorated his country seat.

St Lawrence Church and the Dashwood Mausoleum
The Nefarious Goings On of the Hell Fire Club
WEST WYCOMBE, BUCKINGHAMSHIRE

West Wycombe is a delightful village on the outskirts of which sits West Wycombe Park, the magnificent seat of the Dashwood family. On the summit of the steep conical hill opposite the house is the immense Dashwood Mausoleum, behind which towers the strange golden ball that sits uneasily atop the church of St Lawrence. A series of caves, hewn from the hillside and reached via an entrance that resembles a Gothic church, add to the overall ambience of eccentricity with which the estate is imbued.

The person responsible for all this was Sir Francis Dashwood (1708–81), a man whose name has become a byword for hedonistic debauchery, and who is today best remembered as a leading light in the most infamous of the so-called 'Hell Fire' clubs. These secret societies were once so popular with wealthy aristocrats that in 1721 a royal edict was passed, condemning 'Young People who meet together in the most impious and blasphemous manner… and corrupt the minds and morals of one another.'

Ironically, Dashwood's organization, which operated between the 1740s and the 1760s (and which is now perhaps the only one to be universally remembered) never called itself the 'Hell Fire Club', preferring to be known as the 'Knights of St Francis'. The radical politician John Wilkes (1725–97) – an enthusiastic member – described their gatherings as, 'A set of worthy, jolly fellows, happy disciples of Venus and Bacchus, got together to celebrate women in wine.' The central core of just 13 'apostles', led by Sir Francis Dashwood, included Lord Sandwich, John Wilkes, the painter William Hogarth, poets Charles Churchill, Robert Lloyd and Paul Whitehead, whilst the American Benjamin Franklin was reputed to have been an occasional visitor.

Although their early meetings probably took place at the homes of various members, Sir Francis eventually purchased the ruins of the old Cistercian abbey at nearby Medmenham, and restored it to opulent splendour to provide a more suitable meeting place. Thereafter the society would also be known as 'The Monks of Medmenham'. Despite the fact that the 'brothers' most certainly indulged in a goodly amount of sexual frolicking, and mock religious services, there is no evidence that, as has been frequently claimed, they ever practised Satanism. This suggestion was probably put about by their enemies in the late 18th century, and gathered momentum throughout the next two centuries. There is, however, a delightful though spurious tale that at one of the meetings John Wilkes concealed a baboon, which he had dressed as

sincerely your servant... I never have been half so wicked as I pretended.'

The resulting animosity between them led Lord Sandwich to pursue a vendetta that resulted in Wilkes's expulsion from the House of Commons and his being jailed for three years. At the height of the Wilkes's scandal, Sandwich exclaimed at him, 'Upon my soul Wilkes, I don't know whether you'll die upon the gallows or of the pox.' 'That depends, my lord,' replied Wilkes, 'on whether I first embrace your lordship's principles or your lordship's mistresses.' Their feud also dragged in other members, including Sir Francis, and as a result the society had effectively disbanded by 1766.

WINDSOR GREAT PARK
Herne the Hunter
WINDSOR, BERKSHIRE

There is an old tale goes that Herne the hunter,
Sometime a keeper here in Windsor Forest,
Doth all the winter-time, at still midnight,
Walk round about an oak, with great ragg'd horns,
And there he blasts the tree, and takes the cattle,
And makes milch-kine yield blood, and shakes a chain
In a most hideous and dreadful manner.

ABOVE: In the forests of Windsor Great Park on a windy night, you can still imagine Herne the Hunter leading the Wild Hunt and presaging misfortune on a national scale.

The Merry Wives of Windsor
By William Shakespeare (1564–1616)

the Devil, in a chest beneath his seat. At an appropriate moment, he jerked a cord and opened the chest, whereupon the creature jumped onto Lord Sandwich's shoulders. Believing that he had conjured up the Devil, the terrified Lord Sandwich cried out in alarm, 'Spare me gracious Devil: spare a wretch who never was

'SPARE ME GRACIOUS DEVIL: SPARE A WRETCH WHO NEVER WAS SINCERELY YOUR SERVANT... I NEVER HAVE BEEN HALF SO WICKED AS I PRETENDED.'

LORD SANDWICH PLEADS FOR HIS SOUL

William Shakespeare wrote these lines for Mistress Page in 1597. Despite this being the earliest written reference to the legend of Herne the Hunter, it is probable that Shakespeare was drawing on a much older tradition, the origins of which lay with the Norse god, Odin, and the horned Celtic deity, Cernunnos.

The Wild Hunt, according to myth, was the force behind the ferocious winter tempests that had devastated Europe for as long as man could remember. Primitive peoples were quick to incarnate what they couldn't control. Thus the howling winds were seen as the baying of ghostly hounds, whilst the pounding blizzards were thought of as the hooves of the Wild Hunt's horses galloping overhead. By Shakespeare's day this ancient myth had become established in Windsor Forest. The ghastly entourage had found a local leader in the spectral form of Herne, whom legend says was a huntsman who saved the life of Richard II (1377–99) by throwing himself into the path of a wild stag that was about to maul the king.

As Herne lay fatally wounded, an old man came strolling from Windsor Forest and told Richard that he could save Herne's life. The king ordered the stranger to do what he could and promised that, should Herne recover, he would make him head huntsman. The old man then bound a pair of stag's antlers onto Herne's head and carried him off into the depths of the forest.

The prospect of Herne's promotion so rankled with his fellow huntsmen that they rode into Windsor Forest and, having found the old man's abode, threatened to kill him should their comrade survive. He told them there was nothing he could do to halt the magic, but promised that, although his patient would become head huntsman, he would not hold the position for long. He also warned them that in wishing ill on Herne they had brought his curse upon themselves.

Herne made a full recovery and, just as the king had promised, was made head huntsman. He proved so bad at locating good sport for his royal master, however, that he was dismissed and, in despair, hanged himself from the branch of an oak tree. His fellow huntsmen fared little better as, one by one, they too met with mysterious and violent deaths.

On certain storm-tossed nights, the spectral band of hunters, led by Herne himself and preceded by a pack of baying hounds, are said to gallop through Windsor Great Park, where their appearance is said to always presage a national misfortune or calamity.

St Mary le Bow
Dick Whittington
LONDON

The legend of 'Dick Whittington and his Cat' is one of England's most famous folk tales. Dick was a poor boy, who lived in the days of Edward III and who came to London expecting to find the streets 'paved with gold' and so make his fortune. Unfortunately the best he could manage was employment as a scullion in the kitchen of a wealthy merchant, Mr Fitzwarren. Bullied by the cook, and plagued by the mice and rats that infested his attic, the poor lad was thoroughly miserable. Hoping to deal at least with the latter of his problems, he bought himself a cat, which soon rid his room of the troublesome pests.

When Mr Fitzwarren offered his servants a stake in a cargo of merchandise that was bound for Barbary, Dick had nothing to venture but his cat. His employer accepted the feline investment, and the ship set sail. No sooner had it done so than the cook's harassment intensified and Dick ran away. He

ABOVE: Dick Whittington's cat rid the King of Barbary's palace of its rats, and so became the unwitting cause of Dick's fabulous fortune.

had gone as far as Highgate Hill when, sitting upon on a stone to rest, he heard the bells of Bow Church chiming from the valley below. He fancied he heard them speak, urging him:

Turn again Whittington
Thrice Lord Mayor of London.

He decided to go back. He discovered that the ship had returned, and with it had come a change in his fortunes. The captain of the vessel had arrived in Barbary to find the king's palace overrun with rats. He loaned him Dick's cat, which quickly despatched the vermin, whereupon the grateful monarch purchased the entire cargo for a fantastical sum of money and paid ten times the amount again to buy Dick's cat. Thereafter, Dick Whittington's fortunes went from strength to strength. He married his master's daughter, Alice, and prospered immensely, crowning his achievements by becoming, just as the bells had foretold, three times Lord Mayor of London.

The historical Richard Whittington (1358–1423) was the youngest son of Sir William Whittington, a wealthy Gloucestershire squire. By his early thirties he was a successful London mercer and had married Alice, the daughter the currying of royal favour. He became mayor twice more, in 1406 and 1419, and served as MP for London in 1416.

There is still debate as to the nature of the historical Richard Whittington's cat. The oft-quoted theories that Whittington owed much of his wealth to the coal trade and that colliers were then known as 'cats', or that he had invented the ship known as a 'cat' in which coal was transported in the 18th century, are ingenious though unlikely. The association of his name with a cat was certainly established by Elizabethan times.

Alice Whittington predeceased her husband and, since they had no children, his fortune went to benefit his fellow citizens on his death in 1423. His memory lives on through one of England's best-known fairy tales.

THE EAST END
Jack the Ripper –
The Man Who Never Was
LONDON

At around 3.40am on 31st August 1888, a carter named Charles Cross was walking along Buck's Row, Whitechapel, when he noticed a bundle lying in a gateway. He went to examine it and discovered the body of Mary Nicholls, a 43-year-old prostitute, who had earlier been ejected from a nearby lodging house because she couldn't afford a bed. Moments later another man, Robert Paul, came down the street, and the two men went for the police. They returned with three officers, one of whom, Constable Neil, shone his lantern onto the body and saw that her throat had been cut back to her spine. What no one noticed until later that day was that, beneath her blood-drenched clothing, a deep gash ran along her stomach – she had been disembowelled. Jack the Ripper's reign of terror had begun.

In September 1888 three more prostitutes were found dead and mutilated on the streets of London's East End: Annie Chapman on 8th September, and Elizabeth Stride and Catherine Eddowes in the early hours of 30th September. This 'double murder' led to an intensification of police activity, which brought the killings to a temporary halt. However, the area itself, so the *Star of the East* informed its readers, was 'in a state of ferment and panic. All night long there have been people in the streets, standing round coffee stalls… talking of the latest horrors, and even the men seemed to be in a state of terror.' Despite lurid rumours and several scares, October passed with no further murders. Then, on 9th November,

ABOVE: Jack the Ripper is famous the world over, but his name and legend were the invention of a journalist.

of Sir Ivo Fitzwaryn. By the 1390s he was a master mercer, employing five apprentices and supplying expensive silks, cloth and textiles to the court of Richard II. He had also begun loaning money to the Royal Exchequer and, when the mayor of London died in 1397, the king showed his gratitude by appointing Whittington mayor.

The citizens of London appear to have been more than satisfied, since the following year they re-elected him. When Henry IV deposed Richard II in 1399, Whittington continued to prosper, and such was his importance as a source of ready cash to the Crown that, by the end of Henry's reign, he had lent a total of £21,562. Since usury was illegal at the time, it seems that Whittington's only profit from these loans was

Thomas Bowyer called at the ground-floor room of Miller's Court to collect the overdue rent from 25-year-old Mary Kelly. There was no reply when he knocked on the door, so he pulled aside a curtain that covered a broken window-pane and discovered her mutilated body. Indeed, so horrific were her injuries that she was scarcely recognizable.

At this point, the killings ended as mysteriously as they had begun 12 weeks before. The Whitechapel Murderer had performed his swansong, but the legend of Jack the Ripper was only just beginning. Horrific as the murders were, it is almost certain that, had it not been for the fevered imagination of a journalist, the world at large would have forgotten them long ago. They are remembered today thanks to a letter, purporting to come from the murderer, which was sent to London's central news office towards the end of September 1888. Beginning with the taunt, 'Dear Boss, I keep on hearing that the police have caught me, but they won't fix me just yet', the missive went on to express such boastful sentiments as, 'Grand work the last job was. I gave the lady no time to squeal. How can they catch me now', before ending with the disturbing threat, 'My knife's so nice and sharp I want to get to work right away if I get the chance.'

It was the letter's chilling moniker, 'Jack the Ripper', that turned the lone assassin into the world's first media murderer, as newspapers seized on the name and gave it a huge amount of publicity. In fact, the letter seems likely to have been the work of a journalist. The name he created turned five squalid murders into an international phenomenon, and effectively launched the legend of Jack the Ripper.

LONDON BRIDGE
'London Bridge is Falling Down'
LONDON

In 1013, the Danish leader Sweyn invaded London. He met with a determined resistance, but the citizens eventually surrendered and the English king, Aethelred, fled into exile. The following year Aethelred returned with an ally, Olaf of Norway, and they set about recapturing the city. The Danes, however, repelled the attack, and the invading Norsemen were forced to retreat under a barrage of missiles, coupled with streams of boiling oil and water, that rained upon them from London's heavily fortified bridge.

According to the 13th-century Norse sagas, Olaf's ingenuity saved the day. He had his boats covered with thick platforms of wattle and clay, and with his men ensconced beneath had them row upriver under cover of darkness and tie ropes around the timber piles of the bridge. With the next flood tide, his warriors rowed downriver and brought London Bridge tumbling into the water along with many of the astonished Danish defenders. The rest fled, and the city was taken. This infamous event was later immortalized by the Norse poet Ottar Svarte, who wrote:

> London Bridge is broken down
> Gold is won and bright renown
> Shields resounding
> War horns sounding
> Hildur shouting in the din!
> Arrows singing
> Mailcoats ringing
> Odin makes our Olaf win.

In time, this saga of war evolved into the children's rhyme:

> London Bridge is falling down...My fair lady.

BELOW: Griffins mark the boundaries of the City of London, as they are its legendary guardians. This one can be seen on London Bridge today, set a little way upriver from the bridge that King Olaf pulled down.

ABOVE: Dick Turpin may have visited The Spaniard's Inn, but, since Black Bess was invented by novelist Harrison Ainsworth, it is unlikely that she was stabled here.

THE SPANIARD'S INN
Dick Turpin
HAMPSTEAD HEATH, LONDON

Nestling on the edges of London's Hampstead Heath, the atmospheric Spaniard's Inn is a delightful 16th-century hostelry. In winter months a welcome log fire greets shivering visitors who venture up to the first-floor Turpin's Bar, named for the legend that England's most famous highwayman once stabled his mythical mount, Black Bess, at the inn.

Dick Turpin (1705 –39) is one of those larger-than-life figures whose legend bears little resemblance to his sordid life. Born in the Essex village of Hempstead in September 1705, he grew up in a relatively well-to-do household and received a modest education from the village schoolmaster, James Smith. At the age of 16 he was apprenticed to a butcher in Whitechapel, and five years later set up in business for himself at Waltham Abbey, where he married an innkeeper's daughter named Hester Palmer. He supplemented his income by cattle stealing, but was detected and fled to the wilds of rural Essex. Eventually returning to Epping Forest, he joined a gang of poachers and graduated to burglary. Known as

'Gregory's Gang', their methods were singularly ruthless, and on one occasion Turpin is said to have held the landlady of an inn over her fire until she revealed the whereabouts of her savings. When three of the gang were caught and hanged, the others dispersed.

So Turpin turned his hand to highway robbery. One day in February 1736, on the London to Cambridge Road, he spotted a well-dressed individual, riding a fine horse, and attempted to rob him. His demand to 'Stand and deliver' was, however, met with raucous laughter. 'What, dog eat dog?' guffawed the stranger. Turpin had inadvertently challenged Tom King, known as the 'Gentleman Highwayman'. The two became partners, and, from a cave in Epping Forest, would ride out to rob almost every traveller, rich or poor, that had the misfortune to pass their hideout.

In 1737 Turpin robbed horsedealer Mr Major of his mount – a renowned steeplechaser named White Stocking, on account of its distinctive markings. The horse was instantly recognizable and was spotted at the Red Lion Inn, Whitechapel, where Turpin had stabled it. Major identified it to the local constable, who suggested they keep watch to see who collected the horse. King's brother turned up, was arrested, and offered to take them to his brother and Turpin. The constable and his men surprised the two outlaws, and King was wounded. 'Damn you, shoot or we are taken, Dick!' he cried, whereupon Turpin fired, but accidently shot King's brother. Realizing that his accomplices were beyond help, Turpin abandoned them and made good his own escape.

Four days later, on 7th May, Thomas Morris, a servant of one of the keepers of Epping Forest, spotted Turpin by the entrance to the cave and, borrowing a gun, tried to arrest him. Turpin shot him dead and went on the run, eventually settling in the Yorkshire village of Brough where, calling himself John Palmer, he set up as a cattle and horsedealer. He was accepted into the ranks of the local gentry. In October 1738 he and some friends were returning from a shooting trip when Turpin impulsively shot one of his landlord's gamecocks. Hauled before the local magistrate, he was ordered to find sureties for his good behaviour and, unable to do so, was committed to York Castle prison.

He made the fatal error of writing to his brother-in-law, who was keeping the Bell Inn at Hempstead, to ask for his help. By chance Turpin's former schoolmaster, James Smith, saw the letter and, recognizing the handwriting, alerted the authorities to the fact that 'John Palmer' and Dick Turpin were one and the same. Turpin admitted everything. On 22nd March 1739 he was found guilty of horse stealing and sentenced to death. On the way to his execution he 'bowed repeatedly and with the most astonishing indifference' to the crowds that had turned out to watch.

So how was this psychopathic, thoroughly unpleasant character, transformed into the glamorous figure of popular legend? The answer lies in W. Harrison Ainsworth's immensely popular novel *Rookwood*, published in 1834. Ainsworth's description of Turpin's famous non-stop 370-kilometre (230-mile) ride from London to York, astride his faithful mount, Black Bess, caught the public imagination and turned an average historic novel into a national bestseller. Black Bess was in fact created by Ainsworth, and it was another highwayman, John Nevison (1639–85), who actually made the record-breaking ride more than 20 years before Turpin was born. With the success of *Rookwood*, all this was forgotten and, over the next 50 years, Dick Turpin – housebreaker, torturer and murderer – metamorphosed into Dick Turpin – Prince of Highwaymen.

MARKYATE CELL
The Wicked Lady
MARKYATE, HERTFORDSHIRE

Before the Dissolution of the monasteries, the priory of St Trinity-in-the-Wood occupied the site of Markyate Cell. Thereafter it came into the possession of George Ferrers, one of whose descendents, Lady Katherine Ferrers, would become famous the world over, due largely to Margaret Lockwood's portrayal of her in the 1943 film *The Wicked Lady*.

ABOVE: The previous house on the site of Markyate Cell was once the domain of Lady Katherine Fanshawe, immortalized in the film *The Wicked Lady*.

Born in the late 1630s, Katherine grew up during the English Civil War. At the age of 12 she married her stepbrother, Sir Thomas Fanshawe, who eventually decamped to his family estate in Ireland, leaving his beautiful wife at Markyate Cell to entertain herself. Bored by the traditional pastimes available to the average 17th-century lady, Katherine opted to pursue an altogether more robust hobby and began a secret existence as a highway robber. Each night she would retire to a secret room, concealed behind a kitchen chimney, don the garb of a 'Gentleman of the Road' and, on her huge black horse, set off to rob travellers and coaches on the rutted Hertfordshire byways. The mysterious highwayman became both the talk and the scourge of the district with a ruthless reputation for shooting dead any unfortunate traveller who dared to resist his demands.

Katherine Fanshawe's brutal reign ended on No-man's-land Common, where she held up and murdered a wagoner. Unbeknown to her, two men were hidden amongst the bales of hay on the back of the cart. One of them fired at the masked figure, inflicting a fatal wound. With a scream of pain, Katherine spurred her horse back to the safety of Markyate Cell, where she reached the door to her hidden lair before collapsing. Her servants found her body the following morning.

The legend of the Wicked Lady soon became part of Hertfordshire folklore, and stories of her escapades were handed down from generation to generation. Following her death, her hideaway was reputedly bricked up and successive owners of the property were content to leave it well alone. Indeed, such was her posthumous reputation that, when the old house was destroyed by fire in 1840, it was rumoured that her spirit was responsible for the conflagration.

HOLY TRINITY CHURCH
The Grave of Jack O'Legs
WESTON, HERTFORDSHIRE

Close to the church gateway stand two stones that mark the reputed grave of the fabled local giant, Jack O'Legs. He is said to have lived during the Middle Ages and was supposed to have been so tall that he could lean on first-floor windowsills and chat with occupants inside. He was also renowned for his prowess as an archer, possessing the ability to bring down a bird from almost a kilometre (half a mile) away and to shoot an arrow for over 4.8 kilometres (3 miles).

It was for his nefarious activities as a highway robber that he was best known and, like many an outlaw, was famed for robbing the rich to give to the poor. The rich bakers in the market town of Baldock, who deliberately priced their loaves beyond the means of the poor, were his favourite target. They eventually grew tired of his charitable escapades at their expense, and one day, as he was striding through Baldock, he was hit from behind with a heavy pole and knocked to the ground. Having bound him in chains, the bakers dragged Jack to nearby Gibbet Hill, where they put out his eyes with a red-hot spit. Jack begged to be allowed to fire his bow one last time and asked that his body be buried where the arrow fell. The bakers consented and watched as the arrow flew for over 3 kilometres (2 miles) before striking the spire of Holy Trinity Church in Weston, where it fell into the churchyard. Here, following his execution, he was laid to rest and his grave marked by the two ancient stones, 3.5 metres (12 feet) apart.

THE ABBEY CHURCH OF ST MARY AND ST HELENA
The Pilgrim's Progress
ELSTOW, BEDFORDSHIRE

John Bunyan, the son of a tinker, was christened in the church of St Mary and St Helena on 30th November 1628. He grew up through the troubled years that culminated in the English

ABOVE: Just before his execution, the giant Jack O'Legs was allowed to fire an arrow to locate the spot where his huge frame would be buried at Holy Trinity Church, Weston.

LEFT: It was whilst he was in prison in Bedford gaol for preaching that John Bunyan wrote his most famous work, *The Pilgrim's Progress.*

OPPOSITE: In the days when he cursed and blasphemed, John Bunyan also enjoyed bell ringing at Elstow Church, and later used it as a location in *The Pilgrim's Progress.*

Civil War and, while still in his teens, fought for the Parliamentarians against the Royalists. In 1646 he returned to Elstow and married a local girl with whom he settled down to raise a family, which he supported by working as a tinker. When his wife gave birth to a blind daughter, Bunyan took stock and began to reflect seriously on his life. By his own later admission he had few equals in 'cursing, swearing, lying and blaspheming the Holy name of God.' He began to feel the need to find a deeper purpose in life. He joined a small independent congregation that met at St John's Church, Bedford, and discovered he had a talent for preaching.

With the Restoration of the monarchy in 1660, the authorities, convinced that national unity was only achievable through religious uniformity, forbade independent preachers. John Bunyan, however, refused to be silenced, was arrested and spent 12 years in Bedford gaol. Since he was not a common felon, he was afforded privileges and it was in prison that he composed his famous spiritual allegory *The Pilgrim's Progress.* Several locations around Bedfordshire were incorporated into the narrative, including the abbey church whose bells Bunyan had so delighted in ringing. The closed-up wooden door (that can still be seen at the church's west end) became the 'Wicket Gate' whose keeper is 'named Goodwill', and through which the book's protagonist, Christian, must pass on his journey from the City of Destruction to Mount Zion. The bell tower itself, a little way off from the main body of the church, became the strong castle from which Beelzebub 'and they that are with him, shoot

arrows at them that come up to this gate; if haply they may die before they enter in.'

John Bunyan was released from prison in 1672 and, following a further brief spell of imprisonment, he published his work *The Pilgrim's Progress* in 1678. It was an immediate success and, despite his having written a further 40 books by the time of his death in 1688, it is for this that he is now best remembered.

ECCENTRIC SQUIRES, SILENT GUARDIANS *and* THE FAIRY FOLK

Lives of great men all remind us
We can make our lives sublime,
And departing, leave behind us
Footprints on the sands of time.

FROM *A PSALM OF LIFE*
BY HENRY WADSWORTH LONGFELLOW (1807–1882)

KENT, EAST SUSSEX, WEST SUSSEX & SURREY

T he south-east corner of England, with its green fields, sleepy villages, lush woodlands, rolling downs, wide beaches, high cliffs and bracing coastline, possesses a calm tranquillity that belies its stormy past. For centuries this was the gateway through which passed successive waves of invaders. Celts, Romans, Saxons, Angles, Jutes, Vikings and, finally, Normans, made use of the easy access afforded by the natural harbours that dot the coast. Moving inland, they built fortresses to protect themselves against the next potential invaders; remnants of their defences still lie scattered across the landscape today, lore and legend clinging to their ragged vestiges. In AD597 a peaceful, though more long-lasting, invasion occurred with the arrival from Rome of St Augustine, who built the first church to stand on the site now occupied by Canterbury Cathedral. It is this rich diversity of nation-shaping events that have imbued the region with an almost fabled status in its own right. All this, together with some of England's most stunning vistas, produce a rich profusion of picturesque scenery, fascinating history and legend.

KEY

1. St George's Church
2. St Peter's Church
3. The Church of St Thomas à Becket
4. Windover Hill
5. St Leonard's Forest
6. Chanctonbury Ring
7. The Church of St Mary the Virgin
8. St Peter's Church

ST GEORGE'S CHURCH
Pocahontas
GRAVESEND, KENT

If it were not for a tragic quirk of fate, Pocahontas would never have set foot in Gravesend. As it happens, she came here to die, and was buried in a long-lost grave in St George's church.

Matoaka — to give her correct name — was the spirited daughter of the Indian chieftain, Powhatan, ruler of the land that the English called Virginia. 'Pocahontas' was her childhood nickname and translates as either 'little wanton' or 'the naughty one'. She was around eight years old when her legendary encounter with the English adventurer Captain John Smith took place. According to his account, Smith was captured by a group of Indians in December 1607 and taken before Powhatan. He was forced to lie stretched out on two large flat stones, whilst several warriors stood over him armed with heavy clubs. Suddenly, a little girl hurried over to him and took his 'head in her arms and laid her own upon his to save

PREVIOUS PAGES: In life, 'Mad Jack Fuller' was a man of few pretensions. In death, he was laid to rest in this pretentious pyramid tomb in Brightling churchyard.

LEFT: Pocahontas saves the life of Captain John Smith, by protecting him from a group of Indians that had captured him, and wins her place in legend.

BELOW: The statue of Pocahontas that stands in Gravesend commemorates the fact that she came here to die, and was buried in a grave at St George's Church.

him from death.' The girl was Pocahontas and, thanks to her intervention, Powhatan not only spared Smith's life, but also made him a subordinate chief.

Pocahontas and Smith soon became good friends. She was a regular visitor to the English colony of Jamestown, whose residents she helped save from starvation by bringing supplies of food throughout the winter. However, relations between the Indians and the colonists began to deteriorate the following year, and Pocahontas's visits became less frequent. Then, in October 1609, a gunpowder explosion seriously injured Captain John Smith, and his wounds necessitated his return to England.

In 1612, Captain Samuel Argall, an English colonist, seeing an opportunity to extort concessions and a hefty ransom from Powhatan, lured Pocahontas onto his ship and took her hostage. He sent word to Powhatan that his daughter would only be released if he returned the English prisoners he was holding, plus weapons that the Indians had stolen. Powhatan paid enough to keep negotiations open and then asked that the English take good care of his beloved daughter. Meanwhile Pocahontas, whose first reaction to her dilemma was 'exceeding pensive and discontented', had grown 'accustomed to her captivity.' In April 1613 Argall returned to Jamestown, bringing Pocahontas with him. Shortly afterwards she was moved to the new settlement at Henrico, where she was educated in the Christian faith and fell in love with wealthy widower John Rolfe.

A year later the governor of Henrico, Sir Thomas Dale, gathered a force of about 150 armed men, and sailed with Pocahontas into Powhatan's territory, where he demanded that the full ransom be paid immediately. When the Indians attacked, the English retaliated by destroying several villages and killing a number of natives. Pocahontas was allowed to go ashore and meet with two of her brothers. She told them that she was being well treated and that she wished to marry

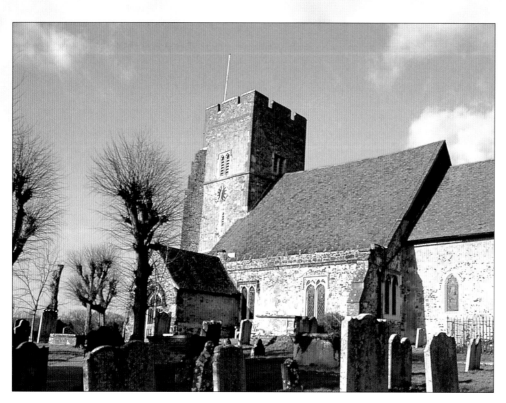

John Rolfe. When word reached Powhatan, he gave his consent to the union and the English departed, elated at the prospect of this potentially peacekeeping marriage. Returning to the colony, Pocahontas was christened Rebecca, and, on 5th April 1614, married John Rolfe. As the English had hoped, a general spirit of goodwill between the colonists and the Indians resulted from the union.

In 1616, hoping to raise further investment in the Virginia company, Sir Thomas Dale sailed for England. To gain publicity he took with him several Indians, including Pocahontas, who was accompanied by her husband and their young son, Thomas. She was presented to King James I, lauded by the great and the good of London society, and caused a sensation wherever she went.

In March 1617, John Rolfe decided to return with his family to Virginia. From the moment they set sail it became apparent that Pocahontas, who was seriously ill with either pneumonia or tuberculosis, would not survive the voyage. She was taken ashore at Gravesend and, as she lay dying, comforted her grieving husband with the words, 'All must die. 'Tis enough that the child liveth.' She died on 22 March 1617, aged just 22, and was then buried in the churchyard of St George's, Gravesend.

ABOVE: The misinterpretation of Dame Dorothy Selby's epitaph in St Peter's Church, Ightham, has given birth to one of Kent's more spurious legends.

BELOW: Did Dame Dorothy Selby, as some believe the inscription on her tomb claims, warn the authorities about the impending Gunpowder Plot?

ST PETER'S CHURCH
The Tomb of Dame Dorothy Selby
IGHTHAM, KENT

A misinterpretation of the inscription on her tomb has resulted in a curious legend about Dame Dorothy Selby. She lived at Ightham Mote and was a talented embroiderer, whose work included elaborate depictions of historical and contemporary events. Two lines of her epitaph in St Peter's Church mention that her 'Arte disclos'd that Plot, which had it taken; Rome had tryumph'd & Britains walls had shaken.' This actually refers to her depiction of the 1605 Gunpowder Plot in embroidery, but legend has placed a more sinister connotation upon the lines.

It was Dame Dorothy, so the story goes, who saved the life of King James I by writing to her cousin, Lord Monteagle, warning him not to attend the opening of Parliament. It was this 'dark and doubtful' letter that exposed the treason and led to the capture of Guido Fawkes. Friends of the conspirators are said to have walled her up alive inside a cupboard at Ightham Mote in revenge for the betrayal.

Dame Dorothy Selby actually died on 15th March 1641 having been pricked by an infected needle. She was buried in the church of St Peter's, Ightham, where a later legend-monger, evidently misunderstanding her inscription, endowed her memory with a pivotal role in one of history's most infamous events.

THE CHURCH OF ST THOMAS À BECKET
The Tomb of John 'Mad Jack' Fuller
BRIGHTLING, EAST SUSSEX

John Fuller (1757–1834), better known to his contemporaries as 'Mad Jack', weighed in at a hefty 140 kilos (22 stone) and was a bluff man of fiery temperament and few pretensions. He contemptuously declined the offer of a peerage, making the remark, 'I was born Jack Fuller and Jack Fuller I'll die.' As Member of Parliament for the district he was forcibly ejected from the house more than once. On one notable occasion he referred to the Speaker as 'the insignificant little fellow in the wig'! Yet he also possessed a philanthropic streak and was instrumental in the founding of the Royal Institute in London, where two Fullerian professorships still commemorate him.

It is, however, his passion for building follies that has proved to be his most enduring legacy, and evidence of that obsession is today scattered about the East Sussex countryside. His masterpiece is undoubtedly the 6-metre (20-foot) high pyramidal mausoleum that he constructed in St Thomas's churchyard, beneath which he was buried. This lasting tribute to his eccentricity sits somewhat uncomfortably alongside the church and legends aplenty swarm around it. One of the reasons he gave for declining a conventional burial was his terror of being eaten by his relatives. 'The worms would eat me,' he explained, 'the ducks would eat the worms and my relatives would eat the ducks.' His body, resplendent in full evening dress and a top hat, was placed sitting in his favourite chair at the centre of the bizarre mausoleum. Before him was a table laid with a magnificent feast, including a bottle of port and a whole roast chicken. On the floor around him was scattered broken glass, so that 'when the Devil comes to claim his own he might at least cut his feet.'

Sadly, this colourful legend was proved untrue when, in 1983, structural repairs necessitated the reopening of the pyramid, which was found to be empty. 'Mad Jack', it transpired, was given a conventional burial beneath the floor of this decidedly unconventional resting place.

BELOW: It was long believed that the body of John Fuller sat before an immense banquet inside this pyramid mausoleum in Brightling churchyard.

WINDOVER HILL
The Legend of the Long Man
NR WILMINGTON, EAST SUSSEX

Few sites in England are more prominent or eye-catching than this remarkable colossus, etched into the green turf of a Sussex hillside. He measures an impressive 72 metres (235 feet) across by 70.5 metres (231 feet) tall, and his origins are shrouded in mystery. Some say that he is of prehistoric origin, others that he is Roman, whilst he has also been attributed to idle monks, whiling away halcyon summer afternoons in the 11th or 12th centuries. There is also evidence to suggest that he is an 18th-century folly. He acquired his present appearance in 1874, when the then owner of the site, the Duke of Devonshire, had him outlined in brick. It is still rumoured that the prudish Victorians used the opportunity of this makeover to rob him of his manhood!

The hillside on which he stands is pocked with indentations caused by ancient flint-mining work. Local tradition, however, has long considered these proof that there lies a fearful legend of battling giants behind the genesis of the Long Man. The titans lived respectively on Windover Hill and nearby Firle Beacon. One day the two quarrelled and began hurling massive boulders at each other. As the rocks thundered into the hillside, they are said to have caused the indentations. Eventually, the Firle giant proved victorious and his opponent fell dead on Windover Hill, where the mighty figure of the Long Man marks the site of his grave. It is possible that behind this colourful tale lies a vague folk memory of an actual battle between two heroes, one of whom was buried in the vicinity.

We will probably never know to what age the Long Man of Wilmington actually belongs or what purpose he originally served. The only certainty is that when we are long gone he will still be here, gazing out across a landscape over which he has watched for centuries.

ST LEONARD'S FOREST
The Lair of Dragons
EAST SUSSEX

Giant serpents and 'wondrous adders' are reputed to have dwelt in the darker recesses of the Sussex countryside as long ago as AD770. The most famous and ferocious of all was the dragon that inhabited the thickly wooded depths of St Leonard's Forest

in the latter years of the 6th century. St Leonard, a holy hermit, was the only man brave enough to battle the fearsome monster and, although he was horribly injured, he finally managed to kill it. The profusion of lilies of the valley that still carpet the forest floor are said to be descended from those that blossomed where the saint's blood fell. In commemoration of St Leonard's bravery, God is said to have decreed that the forest adders would never sting again, and that its nightingales, whose song had proved a constant source of distraction to the holy man's prayers, would be silent forevermore.

It appears, however, that St Leonard failed to rid the forest of all its hideous residents. In 1614 a 'strange and monstrous serpent' was again reported to be terrorizing the district. The creature was said to be almost 3 metres (over 9 feet) long, with a thickset midriff and thin ends. It was covered in red and black scales, had large feet and, on its flanks, 'two great bunches so big as a large footeball, which (as some thinke) will in time grow to wings.' Wherever it went the dragon left in its wake a trail of 'glutinous and slimie matter, which is very corrupt and offensive to the smell.' It was believed to have been responsible for the deaths of a man and a woman whose bodies were found in St Leonard's Forest and who had, apparently, been poisoned by its deadly venom. Although (according to a contemporary pamphlet) it caused a great deal of annoyance, the dragon seems to have disappeared after a few short months, and neither folklore nor legend makes any mention of what became of it.

CHANCTONBURY RING
The Devil's Merry Dance
NR WASHINGTON, WEST SUSSEX

Rising to an impressive height of 239 metres (783 feet) and affording stunning vistas over the surrounding countryside, the Iron Age hill fort of Chanctonbury Ring is a noticeable and dominating landmark that exudes a peculiar air of chilling mystery.

There are many legends and traditions associated with the hill, chief amongst them being the belief that the Devil had a hand in its formation. He is said to have been so annoyed when he discovered that the inhabitants of Sussex were being converted to Christianity, that he endeavoured to drown them by digging a deep trench to the sea. As he dug, clods of earth flew everywhere and landed in untidy heaps across the landscape, one of which became Chanctonbury Ring. Fortunately for the residents of Sussex, a wily old woman who lived nearby set a lighted candle upon her window ledge and placed a polished sieve behind it. This disturbed a cockerel, which began to crow loudly; the Devil, looking up from his work, mistook the candle's reflection in the sieve for the rising sun and fled without completing his task. It is also widely believed that if you run seven times around the summit in an anticlockwise direction on either a dark and moonless night, or during the time it takes the clock to strike midnight, then the Devil will appear and offer you a bowl of milk, soup or porridge. Should you accept, he will either claim your soul, or else grant your dearest wish.

OPPOSITE, ABOVE: When St Leonard killed a ferocious dragon in the forest named for him, God decreed that the adders hereabouts would never sting again.

OPPOSITE, BELOW: One of the most prominent hillside figures, the Long Man of Wilmington has guarded the landscape for centuries and will be there long after we are gone.

BELOW: Run counter-clockwise around the summit of Chanctonbury Ring and the Devil will appear to either claim your soul or grant your dearest wish.

Antiquities of the County of Surrey records a far more colourful tradition behind its origins.

According to Aubrey there was once a particular stone on Borough-hill 'in the parish of Frensham'. If anyone knocked on this stone and declared aloud the name of an item they wished to borrow and stated when they would return it, they would hear a disembodied voice informing them when to come and collect the desired article. The Frensham cauldron, so he records, 'was borrow'd here after the manner aforesaid, but not return'd according to the promise; and though the caldron [sic] was afterwards carried to the stone it could not be receive'd, and ever since that time no borrowing there.'

ST PETER'S CHURCH
Blanche Heriot and the Legend of the Curfew Bell
CHERTSEY, SURREY

The Wars of the Roses were a protracted series of struggles for the Crown of England, fought between the houses of Lancaster and York. Some of the bloodiest skirmishes took place during the feeble reign of the Lancastrian king, Henry VI, who, in 1465, was imprisoned in the Tower of London by his rival, Edward IV. In October 1470 Richard Neville, Earl of Warwick, drove Edward from England and restored Henry to the throne. Six months later, however, Edward was back, and on Easter Sunday 1471 he defeated Warwick at the Battle of Barnet. In the heat of the skirmish, Herrick Evenden, a nephew of Neville's, overpowered a prominent Yorkist soldier, but spared his life. The relieved man gave Evenden his ring as a token of his gratitude.

With the battle lost, Evenden fled the field and sought sanctuary in St Peter's Abbey at Chertsey. Captured by the

THE CHURCH OF ST MARY THE VIRGIN
The Fairy Cauldron
FRENSHAM, SURREY

Inside the 14th-century church of St Mary the Virgin at Frensham is an immense cauldron, which in former times may well have been used to hold the vast quantities of ale required to slake the thirsts of parishioners at village feasts. John Aubrey (1626–97) in his *Natural History and*

Yorkists, he was sentenced to death, his execution to be carried out when Chertsey's curfew bell tolled. Hoping that his earlier act of mercy would save his life, Evenden despatched a rider to take the ring to Edward IV and seek a pardon. The king duly approved a reprieve, but the messenger was delayed on his return and, with the curfew about to toll, still had a mile left to ride. Evenden's lover Blanche Heriot saved the day by climbing into the belfry and hanging onto the clapper of the bell to prevent the curfew from being sounded. By the time the soldiers had investigated, the messenger had arrived and Herrick Evenden was a free man.

ABOVE: Had Blanche Heriot not hung onto the clapper of St Peter's curfew bell in Chertsey, her lover Herrick Evenden would most certainly have been executed at its first chime.

RIGHT: Richard Neville – 'Warwick the Kingmaker' – was killed at the Battle of Barnet on Easter Sunday, 1471.

HELLISH HOUNDS
and the WRATH of a
QUEEN

Nay, come up hither. From this wave-wash'd mound
Unto the furthest flood-brim look with me;
Then reach on with thy thought till it be drown'd.
Miles and miles distant though the last line be,
And though thy soul sail leagues and leagues beyond,
Still, leagues beyond those leagues, there is more sea.

FROM *THE CHOICE*
BY DANTE GABRIEL ROSSETTI (1828–1882)

ESSEX, CAMBRIDGESHIRE, SUFFOLK & NORFOLK

T he eastern counties of England occupy the region that once formed the ancient Kingdom of East Anglia, whose inhabitants consisted of the North Folk (Norfolk) and the South Folk (Suffolk). Bounded to the west by the swamps of the Fens, buffered to the east and north by the sea, and hemmed in at the south by the thick woodlands of Saxon Essex, it was for centuries a distant and mysterious region, populated by a hardy and resourceful people. Successive waves of invaders managed to breach its natural defences, and Romans, Angles, Saxons, Vikings and Danes have all left their mark upon the landscape. The more peaceful incursions made by Icelandic fishermen, Flemish weavers and Dutch drainage specialists have in turn left their imprint on the region's agriculture, trades and skills. This secluded corner of rural England has also influenced the history of the nation. Among the famous who hailed from here are: Hereward the Wake, Lord Nelson, Boadicea, Cardinal Wolsey, Oliver Cromwell and the Boleyn family. In short, it is a landscape that has both fostered and bred legends. Its varied scenery imbues a genuine sense of isolation.

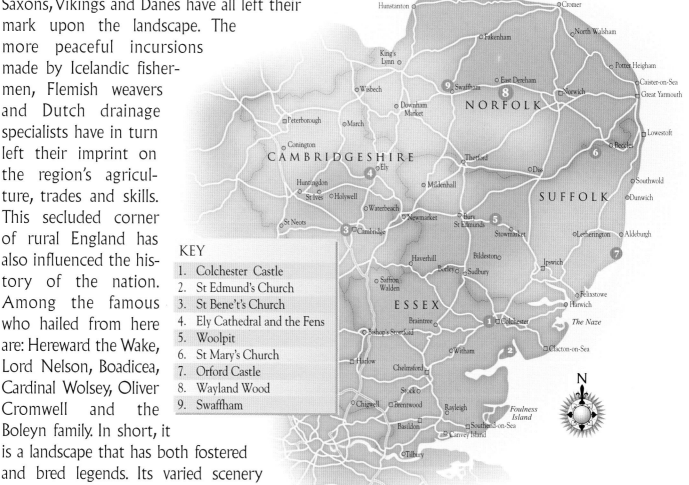

KEY

1. Colchester Castle
2. St Edmund's Church
3. St Bene't's Church
4. Ely Cathedral and the Fens
5. Woolpit
6. St Mary's Church
7. Orford Castle
8. Wayland Wood
9. Swaffham

COLCHESTER CASTLE
Boudica's Revenge
COLCHESTER, ESSEX

Deep below the ground in parts of London, Colchester or St Albans, lies a stratum of reddish-brown ash, peppered with scorched pieces of Roman pottery, which archaeologists call 'Boudica's layer'. It is the only physical evidence of a ferocious rebellion that very nearly changed the course of British history as we know it.

The infamous woman behind the firestorm is an historical enigma about whom very little is actually known. Even the spelling and pronunciation of her name are subject to considerable debate. Boudica is probably the most accurate; Boadicea is certainly the best known. In the Celtic language of the Iceni tribe of Norfolk, whose leader she was, her name simply meant 'Victory'.

When the Emperor Claudius ordered the invasion of Britain in AD43, Boudica's husband Prasutagus was one of the many tribal leaders who agreed to become a client king of Rome. This pragmatic submission left him as ruler of his people whilst affording him the comforts that came with

ABOVE: Colchester Castle stands on the site of the Roman temple of Claudius, where the citizens were incinerated in Boudica's rebellion.

PREVIOUS PAGES: When Roman soldiers abused the Iceni Queen Boudica and her two daughters they sparked a rebellion that almost ended the occupation of Britain.

being a part of the Empire. When he died in AD60, Prasutagus left half his estate to the Roman emperor (now the infamous Nero) and the other half to his wife and their two teenage daughters. Rome's local administrator declared Boudica's tribal lands a slave province and sent troops to her palace. They seized Boudica, raped her daughters, and submitted the Queen of the Iceni to the humiliation of a public flogging. Their actions turned a willing collaborator into an implacable enemy and lit a flame of resentment that cost the lives of more than 100,000 people and almost lost the Romans their foothold in Britain.

Boudica's revenge was well planned and ruthlessly executed. First she forged an immense alliance of disaffected tribes and then waited until the cream of the Roman army, under their commander Seutonius Paulinus, was far way, suppressing the last

ABOVE: Was Sarah Wrench really a teenage witch? Her grave, covered in an iron cage, seems to imply that the local parishioners wanted to stop her leaving her grave.

Druid stronghold on the island of Anglesey. Then she hit back. With a vast army of some 120,000 tribesmen, she rampaged across eastern England, torching Roman settlements en route for the ultimate symbol of Roman occupation, Camulodunum (Colchester). The ill-prepared residents, consisting largely of retired soldiers and their families, managed to hold out for two days, and sent messengers to Londinium (London) imploring the Procurator, Decianus, to provide reinforcements. He did so, dispatching a paltry 200 soldiers, who were quickly overcome. Camulodunum's surviving citizens retreated to their temple where, for two more days, they cowered behind its thick walls. We can only guess at the final agonies of the thousands of unfortunate colonists, as the searing heat of Boudica's revenge incinerated them.

'LOOK ROUND AND VIEW YOUR NUMBERS. BEHOLD THE DISPLAY OF WARLIKE SPIRITS AND CONSIDER THE MOTIVES FOR WHICH WE DRAW THE AVENGING SWORD. ON THIS SPOT WE MUST EITHER CONQUER, OR DIE WITH GLORY.'

BOUDICA'S SPEECH BEFORE HER WARRIORS

The Roman 9th Legion, based in Lincoln, had already been despatched to relieve Camulodunum, but the Britons ambushed them en route and annihilated the infantryman, leaving the demoralized cavalry to retreat to their base. When news of this humiliating defeat reached Procurator Decianus, he gathered his entire staff and fled to Gaul.

With Boudica's forces snowballing towards Londinium, Suetonius Paulinus ordered his troops to return and rode on ahead, hoping to save the city. He realized that it would be impossible to defend, however, and headed north to rendezvous with his army, leaving London at the mercy of an insatiable horde of native fury that fired the buildings and slaughtered the remaining inhabitants.

The settlement of Verulamium (St Albans) was next to feel the wrath of Boudica's revenge en route to an inevitable confrontation with the army of Seutonius Paulinus. We know virtually nothing about the ensuing battle; common consensus is simply that it was somewhere in the West Midlands. The Roman historian, Tacitus, records only that Suetonius sought a site that would assist his heavily outnumbered soldiers and settled on 'a spot encircled with woods, narrow at the entrance, and sheltered in the rear by a thick forest.' An open plain lay before him, thus ensuring that the enemy could only attack from one direction.

As the rebel force amassed for the final battle, so too did their families, taking up position behind the warriors to cheer and applaud the victory that they were sure was theirs.

Boudica, with her two daughters, drove through their ranks in her chariot. 'Look round and view your numbers,' she is said to have told them. 'Behold the display of warlike spirits and consider the motives for which we draw the avenging sword. On this spot we must either conquer, or die with glory.' Seutonius, meanwhile, was imploring his soldiers to, 'Keep your ranks; discharge your javelins; rush forward to a close attack and hew a passage with your swords. Pursue the vanquished, and never think of spoil or plunder. Conquer, and victory gives you everything.'

As the screeching throng of Britons came rushing towards them, the Romans held their ground in a tight phalanx. Seutonius waited until his opponents were within range and then gave the order to attack. A volley of javelins hailed down upon the Britons, followed by a wave of infantry and cavalry who charged into their ranks and cut them down en masse. The surviving rebels turned to run, but found their way blocked by their own families. The Romans closed in, and the gory fracas that followed saw men, women and children hacked to pieces. Boudica is said to have poisoned herself and was buried by her people at a secret location, that some claim now lies deep beneath Platform 10 of King's Cross railway station!

ST EDMUND'S CHURCH
Sarah Wrench, the Teenage Witch
EAST MERSEA, ESSEX

East Mersea is an unspoilt sea-sprayed island in whose churchyard is a curious tomb on which a weathered inscription commemorates Sarah Wrench. She was 15 years old when she died on 6th May 1848, and aside from that, little is known about her. Over her grave the parishioners placed a bizarre iron cage. It is this, coupled with the fact she lies buried on the church's north side — typically the unconsecrated part where suicides and felons were placed — that has led to a belief that she was a witch. Indeed, it is claimed that in life she was so feared that the inhabitants felt compelled to place this iron cage over her to stop her leaving the grave and troubling the neighbourhood.

ST BENE'T'S CHURCH
Thomas Hobson
CAMBRIDGE, CAMBRIDGESHIRE

Thomas Hobson (1544–1630) lies buried in an unmarked grave somewhere within the precincts of this delightful little church in the centre of the bustling university town of Cambridge. In 1568 he inherited his father's cart and eight

ABOVE: Thomas Hobson is buried at St Bene't's Church. He is remembered the world over as the inspiration behind the saying 'Hobson's Choice'.

horses and began transporting all manner of goods between Cambridge and London. University mail, students, tradesmen, clerics and even live fish for the royal household bounced along the rough highways of 16th-century England aboard Thomas Hobson's cart. His hard work paid off and very soon he had expanded his business into the renting of horses, offering a stable of 40 beasts for use by Cambridge undergraduates.

With such a wide variety of horses to choose from, many was the wealthy patron who thought his money could secure him the best. Thomas Hobson was adamant that his clients always took the horse nearest the stable door, thus ensuring that every customer was treated alike and every horse was ridden an equal number of times. If anyone argued, Hobson would curtly inform them, 'This one or none'. It wasn't long before the phrase 'Hobson's Choice' had passed into common usage to describe a situation where no real choice was available. Thomas Hobson thus became one of those people whose name is famous the world over, despite many who use it having no idea who he was and when or where he lived.

ELY CATHEDRAL AND THE FENS
Hereward the Wake
THE ISLE OF ELY, CAMBRIDGESHIRE

ABOVE: Hereward the Wake exacts a terrible vengeance on the Norman invaders who had murdered his brother.

Although the draining of the fens in the 18th century ended Ely's insularity, officially it is still an island. Despite its now being surrounded by some of the finest arable land in the country, there are times, especially when heavy mists creep across the low-lying fields, when it is possible to imagine that the ancient marshlands are still the abode of England's most famous freedom fighter, Hereward the Wake.

Not much is known about Hereward the Wake (meaning 'wary'). He is thought to have been a Saxon who led a dissolute life as a youth and was consequently exiled by his father. While he was abroad, William the Conqueror invaded and Hereward returned to find his family estates in Norman hands, and the head of his slain brother displayed on a spike over the gate of their house. Descending on the usurpers, he slew every one of them and, next day, the heads of 14 Normans had replaced that of his brother.

Hereward became the leader of a group of Saxon warriors who, from the fortified Isle of Ely, conducted a brutally effective guerrilla campaign against the Normans. Thanks to the impassibility of the surrounding fens, their base was unreachable without knowledge of the secret pathways that led through the treacherous marshes.

William the Conqueror, determined to root out this pocket of Anglo-Saxon resistance, ordered a wooden causeway to be built across the fens and enlisted the assistance of a French witch whom he placed in a high wooden tower. As she was trundled over the jetty towards Ely, she screamed terrible curses at the rebels. Hereward had disguised himself as a workman, and no sooner had the Norman troops set off across the timber causeway, than he had set fire to it. Fanned by the fenland winds, the flames raced through the reeds, fired the tower and the witch fell to her death. The panic-stricken Normans were either picked off by the arrows of Saxon marksmen, or fled blindly into the marshes, where hundreds of them perished.

In 1071 the monks of the abbey at Ely grew tired of the constant siege and showed the Normans the secret pathway through the fens. Although Hereward managed to escape, and may have kept up his guerrilla campaign for a time, the resistance to Norman occupation was effectively over and Hereward, accepting the inevitable, is reputed to have finally sworn allegiance to William at Winchester.

ABOVE: The graceful walls of Ely Cathedral, whose monks betrayed Hereward the Wake to the Normans and ended his guerrilla campaign.

LEFT: Mystery and magic cling to the primeval vestiges of Wicken Fen that once surrounded the fortified Isle of Ely.

WOOLPIT
The Green Children
WOOLPIT, SUFFOLK

The sign of this peaceful little village, in the heart of rural Suffolk, commemorates one of the most curious legends to emerge from the mists of medieval history. The story was chronicled by two 13th-century clerics, Ralph, Abbot of Coggleshall, and William of Newburgh. One summer, during the reign of King Stephen (1135–54), farmworkers bringing in the harvest from the surrounding fields were surprised by two strange figures emerging out of the nearby pits: a boy and girl, whose skins were completely green. They wore strange-looking clothes, could not understand anything that the villagers said, but seemed able to converse with each other in a strange, unintelligible tongue. The bemused villagers took the children to the home of the local landowner, Sir Richard de Calne. They refused to eat any food until some green beans were offered, and these they consumed hungrily.

The boy soon died, but the girl quickly settled into her new surroundings where, having adapted to a normal diet, her skin gradually lost its green hue and she became like any other woman. She was soon able to converse in English and answer her host's questions. She said that she and her brother had dwelt previously in a place called St Martin's land, where the sun never shone. Its residents, she said, lived in perpetual twilight, although they could see another 'land of light' across a river. One day, she and her brother had been tending their father's sheep, when they heard the beautiful sound of bells and had entered an underground passageway in search of their source. Emerging from the darkness, they had been overcome by a dazzling light and had lain motionless for a time. Startled by those who found them, they had attempted to escape, but were unable to find the entrance to the cavern again and so had been brought to the house where she now resided. In time, the girl married a man from King's Lynn, and went on to live a long and happy life, leaving behind her a curious enigma over which people have been pondering ever since.

ST MARY'S CHURCH
Black Shuck
BUNGAY, SUFFOLK

On 4th August 1577 a 'Straunge and terrible Wunder' occurred at the church of St Mary's, Bungay. As the morning service began, a fearsome tempest suddenly blew up outside the building. Lightning streaked across the heavens and great rolls of thunder shook the church to its foundations. Moments later the doors flew open and a hideous black dog burst in upon the alarmed parishioners. It raced along the

aisle with 'greate swiftnesse and incredible haste' and, as it
moved between two members of the congregation, the others watched in horror as the demon 'wrung the necks of
them bothe.' The hound brushed against another onlooker
rendering him 'as shrunken as a piece of leather left in a hot
fire.' At more or less the same time, the creature also paid a
visit to nearby Blythburgh Church, where he killed three
parishioners and left deep claw marks on the north door,
which are still visible today.

Those who witnessed these terrible happenings knew that
they had seen the Black Dog or demon hound. Although this
fearsome spectre haunts the darker recesses of the local consciousness in many parts of Britain, it is to the bleak expanse
of the East Anglian coastline and the untamed stretches of its
wild fens that its legend clings most vigorously. He arrived
here with the Viking invaders who brought with them tales of
Odin's hounds. The Anglo-Saxons singularized them, and thus

was born the legend of Black Shuck — a name derived from
their word *succa*, meaning demon — the moniker by which the
dreaded creature has been known in these parts for over
1,000 years. At some stage, long ago, he managed to spring
from the realm of fantasy and came bounding onto the East
Anglian byways, a living, breathing hound of hell, able to strike
terror and death into those who have been unfortunate
enough to cross his fearsome path.

ORFORD CASTLE
The Wild Man of Orford
ORFORD, SUFFOLK

There is little today to suggest what a prosperous port Orford
once was, save the ruins of its mighty castle built in 1165 by
Henry II. It was to this imposing fortress in 1204 that a group
of agitated fishermen brought a most remarkable catch.
Having spent a day trawling the waters off the Suffolk coast,
they noticed that their nets were unusually heavy, and they
discovered a strange creature caught up amongst the fish.

ABOVE: Suffolk's Wayland Wood has long been reputed to be the place where the famous Babes in the Wood were left to die by their uncle.

It resembled a man, but its naked body was covered with hair; it had a long, shaggy beard and a bald crown atop its head. Over the days that followed, the castle governor, Bartholomew de Gladville, attempted to communicate with his strange prisoner, but to no avail. Apart from a few grunts, the Wild Man of Orford, as he became known, would say nothing. They fed him a diet of raw fish from which he would always wring out the moisture before eating. They even took him to a service at Orford Church, and were perturbed to discover the

sacraments meant nothing to him. However, he seemed relatively happy at the castle, and did not attempt to escape, even when he was taken out to sea for a swim. After a few months he began to grow restless. One day, when his guardians took him for his customary swim, he slipped beneath the surface and was never seen again.

WAYLAND WOOD
The Babes in the Wood
NR WATTON, NORFOLK

In 1595 Thomas Millington of Norwich published a famous ballad with the catchy title 'The Norfolk Gent. His Will and Testament and howe he committed the keeping of his children to his own brother, who delte most wickedly with them and how God plagued him for it.' Thankfully for generations of pantomime-goers the ballad has been handed down to posterity under the less tongue-tying designation of 'The Babes in the Wood'.

Soon after publication the story became indelibly linked with the creepy rural backwater of Norfolk's Wayland Wood. Here the ancient hazels and gnarled oaks that tower over muddy pathways still look much as they would have 500 years ago. It is an eerie and chilling place where you feel a fear so primeval that you constantly have to resist the almost irrepressible urge to look behind you.

The story begins at nearby Griston Hall, a rambling, red-brick farmhouse dating from 1597. A small brother and sister were left in the care of their uncle by their dying parents. They were, so their father's will stipulated, to inherit the princely sum of £800, but only when they came of age. In the meantime they were to reside with their uncle at Griston Hall. Their uncle, however, determined to rob them of their inheritance, and hired two ruffians to take the children to Wayland Wood and murder them. One of the men was unable to carry out such a callous crime and, when he failed to persuade his friend to let the children live, murdered him instead. Promising to return with food, he hid the children deep inside the wood, but he never came back. The children died in each other's arms, whereupon robins covered them with leaves.

Wayland Wood, which also became known as 'Wailing Wood', was quickly established as the scene of the tragedy. When, in August 1879, the old oak under which the children are supposed to have died was struck by lightning and destroyed, people came from miles around to collect souvenirs from it.

SWAFFHAM
The Swaffham Tinker
NORFOLK

That John Chapman was a wealthy 15th-century citizen of the busy market town of Swaffham is a fact upon which both history and legend agree. That he was a generous parishioner, whose money provided the means to build the north aisle and tower of the town's church, is also undisputed. It is upon the source of his wealth that the two disagree. History favours his having being a successful and respected merchant who made his fortune in the uninspiring world of commerce. Legend, on the other hand, has chosen to remember him as a poor tinker who came by his riches courtesy of a prophetic dream.

One night, so the story goes, Chapman dreamt that if he were to go to London and stand upon the bridge, he would meet a man who would tell him how to make his fortune. Struck by both the intensity of the vision and the fact that he had little to lose, Chapman packed a handful of provisions and walked to London, where he took up his position on London Bridge. For three days he stood there, but was rewarded with only amused glances from indifferent citizens. As he was regretting his obvious stupidity, a shopkeeper appeared from the doorway of one of the shops that lined the bridge, and asked what he was doing. Chapman poured out the tale of his dream and lamented allowing himself to be sent on a fool's errand. 'Alas good friend,' said the shopkeeper, 'you are indeed a fool to be led by a dream. I myself have these past nights dreamt that, if I were to go to a place called Swaffham and dig beneath a tree in the garden of a man named John Chapman, I would uncover a vast treasure that was buried there.' Commenting that, 'Only a fool would make such a journey', the man shook his head, laughed and went back into his shop.

Chapman raced home as fast as his legs would carry him and immediately began digging beneath the only tree in his garden. He had not gone far when he struck a large brass pot full of coins. On it there was a Latin inscription, which translated as 'Under me doth lie another much richer than I.' Digging deeper, he found a much larger pot crammed with gold, jewels and coins.

The parish register certainly lists a wealthy citizen, John Chapman, as being a churchwarden in 1462. William White in

ABOVE: The effigy of John Chapman, the 'Swaffham Tinker', on the town's market cross reminds us all that it is sometimes wise to follow our dreams.

his *Gazetteer and History of Norfolk* published in 1845 was, however, quick to pour scorn upon the legend. According to him, the story was 'undoubtedly fabricated by the vulgar, from the rebuses on his name, carved on his seat in the north aisle, representing a peddler or chapman with his pack, and his wife looking over the door of a shop; but this and many other carved seats were removed many years ago.' As far as local folklore is concerned, however, John Chapman will always be remembered as the 'Swaffham Tinker'. A modern wooden effigy depicting him thus stands proudly alongside the town's market cross, a reminder that sometimes it is a wise man who follows his dreams.

Merrie Sherwood, Saintly Maidens, Vanquished Kings and Hounds of the Night

So it is: yet let us sing,
Honour to the old bow-string!
Honour to the bugle-horn!
Honour to the woods unshorn!
Honour to the Lincoln green!
Honour to the archer keen!
Honour to tight Little John,
And the horse he rode upon!
Honour to bold Robin Hood,
Sleeping in the underwood!
Honour to Maid Marian,
And to all the Sherwood-clan!
Though their days have hurried by.

FROM *ROBIN HOOD*
BY JOHN KEATS (1795–1821)

WEST MIDLANDS, LEICESTERSHIRE, NORTHAMPTONSHIRE, NOTTINGHAMSHIRE & LINCOLNSHIRE

The counties that stretch from the Lincolnshire coast to the flat arable pastures of the East and West Midlands have, over the millennia, been home to sundry peoples. Celts, Romans and Vikings have all left their mark both upon the varied landscape and the folk tradition of the region. The Danes came and took the land to the north-east of the Roman Watling Street, which they held for three centuries; as a result, the area became known as the 'Danelaw'. Elsewhere there are constant reminders of some of England's most famous legendary figures and events. Who can wander the byways of Nottinghamshire without giving a thought to the world's most famous outlaw, Robin Hood? Who can gaze out across the windy expanse of Bosworth Field and not ponder the fate of Richard III? On a forlorn mound in Northamptonshire, Scottish thistles still grow upon the site of Fotheringay Castle, where Mary, Queen of Scots, was executed, whilst in the centre of Coventry a statue on horseback commemorates Lady Godiva's famous ride through the city.

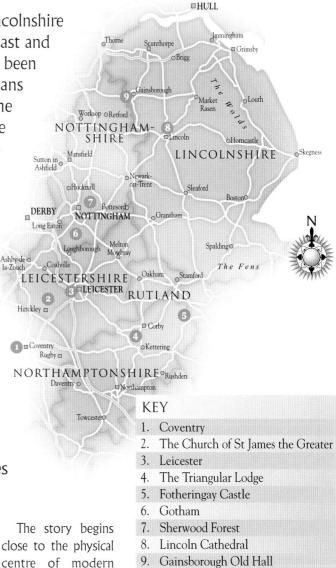

KEY
1. Coventry
2. The Church of St James the Greater
3. Leicester
4. The Triangular Lodge
5. Fotheringay Castle
6. Gotham
7. Sherwood Forest
8. Lincoln Cathedral
9. Gainsborough Old Hall

COVENTRY
Lady Godiva
COVENTRY, WEST MIDLANDS

Unlike many whose names have become synonymous with legend, there is no doubt that Lady Godiva actually existed. The Domesday Book of 1086 records that Godgifu, the name by which she would have been known, was a substantial landowner in her own right and was married to one of the most powerful noblemen of the day, Leofric, Earl of Chester.

The story begins close to the physical centre of modern Coventry, where stand the bombed-out remnants of the once-mighty cathedral. It was around here in 1043 that Leofric and Godiva founded a monastery, which soon became one of the richest in the land.

Leofric took control of Coventry's finances and initiated a series of magnificent public works, the costs of which were borne by the townsfolk through relentless taxation. Lady Godiva, meanwhile, was attempting to raise their aesthetic awareness and was mystified why the rough and ready peasantry appeared unable to appreciate her artistic vision. When she discovered that Leofric's excessive taxes were responsible, she insisted that he reduce them.

At first he refused, but Godiva began nagging Leofric so incessantly that eventually he acceded to her wishes – but on one condition. He argued that since the ancient Greeks and Romans considered the naked human body the pinnacle of nature's perfection, his wife should take her artistic crusade to its logical conclusion and ride naked through Coventry's market place. If she would do this, he in turn would reduce the unpopular taxes. To his astonishment his modest and religious wife accepted the challenge.

So it was that, on the appointed day, at the appointed hour – flanked by two fully-clothed horsewomen – Lady Godiva removed her clothing, mounted her steed, and cantered proudly into the realm of legend. Her long hair fell across her body and veiled it so thoroughly that, despite the fact that most of the populace had turned out to watch, none saw anything, apart from her face and 'fair legs'. Leofric was so amazed by this miracle that, instead of simply reducing taxes, he abolished them altogether.

It is doubtful that the real Lady Godiva ever undertook an artistic streak for the benefit of the good citizens of Coventry. Indeed, the earliest written accounts of the event occur some 200 years after it supposedly happened and, over the centuries, the story has been rewritten to arrive at the version that we know today. Thus, by the 16th century, Lady Godiva was said to have sent messengers around the town asking everyone to stay indoors and shutter their windows at the appointed hour. Because of her popularity, and because they stood to gain from her actions, the citizens willingly obliged.

A hundred or so years later, the antiquarian William Camden visited Coventry and was shown a wooden effigy that inspired him to introduce another character into the legend. Today that same time-worn figure stands, encased in glass, on the first floor of the Cathedral Lane shopping centre. Its blinded eyes and anguished expression are those of a man whose true identity has long been forgotten. By the time Camden came to write him into the story in the late 17th century, he had assumed a name that is now as famous as that of Godiva herself. He is said to be Peeping Tom, the boy who was struck blind when he ignored the good lady's wishes, and snuck a brief peek as she rode proudly by in all her natural glory.

PREVIOUS PAGES: Despite his original legend being associated with Yorkshire's Barnsdale Forest, it is the wooded glades of Nottingham's Sherwood Forest that have now claimed Robin Hood as their own.

BELOW: Coventry's statue of its most famous daughter, Lady Godiva, commemorates her naked ride through the city's streets.

THE CHURCH OF ST JAMES THE GREATER
The Death of King Richard III
DADLINGTON, LEICESTERSHIRE

ABOVE: Those killed at the Battle of Bosworth were buried where Dadlington's Church of St James the Greater now stands in commemoration of their sacrifice.

On 21st August 1485, Richard III led his army out of Leicester and crossed the bridge over the River Soar. With 12,000 men, he was preparing to fight off a challenge to his throne from a force of 5,000 led by the Welsh Henry Tudor, Earl of Richmond. While on the bridge, Richard's foot struck against a protruding piece of wood, whereupon a blind beggar is said to have prophesied 'His head shall strike that pile as he returns.'

Despite commanding a numerically superior force, Richard was relying upon the support of several nobles whose loyalty was questionable. Chief amongst these were the Stanley brothers, William and Thomas, both of whom were viewed as his supporters, despite the latter being married to Margaret Beaufort, mother of Henry Tudor. Furthermore, Thomas's son, Lord Strange — whom Richard was holding hostage to ensure his father's co-operation — had attempted to escape and, under questioning, had confessed that his uncle, William, was planning to betray the king. To add to Richard's worries, the Earl of Northumberland insisted that his men were exhausted

after their long march south and would do better service in the rear, rather than in the thick of the fighting. It was against this background of intrigue that Richard spent the eve of the battle encamped opposite his opponent above the plain of Redemore, near Bosworth.

At dawn on 22nd August 1485, Richard Plantagenet, King of England, donned his armour of burnished steel, mounted his white horse and prepared to do battle. His sleep had been marred by dark dreams and he looked paler than usual. The absence of a chaplain to say mass was, he told his troops, deliberate. If God was on their side then prayers were unnecessary; if not, they were idle blasphemy. He sent a messenger to Lord Thomas Stanley, whose troops were on a ridge to his left, and commanded him to join the royal army if he valued his son's life. Stanley replied that he felt disinclined to do so and, anyway, he had other sons. Richard ordered Lord Strange's immediate execution, but thought better of it and instead placed him under close guard. Richard's advisers begged him to remove his crown, since it would make him a visible target. Replying that he would live or die as King of England, Richard spurred his horse forward, and rode to meet his Welsh challenger.

The battle that followed is one of the worst documented in English history and no eyewitness accounts of it have survived. Even the exact site of the encounter is the subject of intense debate. What we do know is that it lasted just two hours, and was fought on Redemore Plain, an open space of marshy ground surrounded by hills, from which the Stanley brothers and the Earl of Northumberland watched and failed to intervene on the king's behalf. Richard's loyal supporters, the Duke of Norfolk and Lord Ferrers, were slain in the fierce hand-to-hand combat, and the king's advisers begged him to flee, but Richard refused.

Then a messenger pointed out a group of horsemen cantering across the plain towards Sir William Stanley, waving the banner of the red dragon, the standard of Henry Tudor. Realizing that his opponent was attempting to win the Stanley's support, Richard mounted his horse and, with his household cavalry, charged towards the Tudor guards in a bold attempt to kill Henry. He plunged into the enemy ranks with such menacing ferocity that, despite his slight stature, he succeeded in cutting down the immensely strong Sir John Cheney and killing Henry's standard-bearer, William Brandon. Just as Richard came within reach of his goal, Sir William Stanley threw his support behind Henry and brought his troops into the fray. Severely outnumbered, Richard fought bravely on. Unhorsed, he raised his sword and made a last desperate bid to reach his opponent, but the combined Tudor and Stanley forces fell upon him and beat him to the ground. 'Treason! Treason!' he is said to have screamed as he was hacked to death. Sir William Stanley, so legend claims, then retrieved Richard's crown from beneath a nearby thorn bush and, placing it on Henry Tudor's head, proclaimed him King of England.

Richard's blood-encrusted body was stripped naked and, with a felon's halter around his neck, the last King of England to die in battle was tied over the back of a horse and conveyed ignominiously back to Leicester. As the procession crossed over the bridge, his head swung against the protruding wooden block, thus fulfilling the prophecy of the blind beggar.

BELOW: The tale of King Lear's attempt to discover which of his three daughters loved him the most provided inspiration for one of Shakespeare's greatest tragedies.

LEICESTER
The Legend of King Lear
LEICESTERSHIRE

Following the untimely death of Bladud (see page 32) his son, Leir, ascended the throne and ruled for 60 years. Legend holds that he founded a city upon the River Soar and called it Caer Leir, which, in English, became Leicester. According to Geoffrey of Monmouth's *History of the Kings of Britain* Leir had three daughters — Gonorilla, Regan and Cordeilla — of whom he was dotingly fond. His favourite was the youngest, Cordeilla.

In his old age, Leir wished to learn which daughter loved him the most in order that she might inherit the largest share of his kingdom. Gonorilla claimed to love him more than her very soul, whilst Regan vowed that she loved him more than anyone else on earth. Suitably flattered, Leir turned to his youngest daughter who told him that she loved him as any daughter would a father, and that 'just as you are worth whatever you possess, so I love you for what you are.' Presuming that Cordeilla valued him only for his possessions, Leir disinherited her.

Leir married his two eldest girls to the Dukes of Cornwall and Albany, and arranged for them to share his kingdom after his death. Having heard of her beauty, Aganippus, King of the Franks, agreed to take Leir's ungrateful youngest daughter without land or dowry, and Cordeilla was despatched to Gaul to become his wife.

Within a few years, Gonorilla and Regan had contrived to rid their father of his followers and kingdom, forcing him to

EYGENTLICHE ABBILDVNG WIE ETTLICH ENGLISCHE EDELLEVT EINEN RAHT schließen den König sampt dem gantzen Parlament mit Pulfer zuvertilgen.

Robert Winter · *Bates* · *Christopher Wright* · *Iohn wright* · *Thomas Percy* · *Guido Fawkes* · *Robert Catesby* · *Thomas Winter*

ABOVE: Although Guido Fawkes is now the name most associated with the Gunpowder Plot, it was Robin Catesby (second from right) who conceived and led the scheme.

OPPOSITE: Rushton's Triangular Lodge was built by fervent Catholic Sir Thomas Tresham, and stands as a unique, though bizarre, testimony to the zeal of his faith.

sail for Gaul, where he hoped that Cordeilla would forgive him. She was overjoyed to see her father. Her husband provided an army with which Leir regained his throne and ruled for three more years before his death. Cordeilla buried him in a vault beneath the River Soar and, succeeding to his throne, reigned for five years before her sisters' sons revolted and deposed her. Imprisoned by her nephews, she sunk into despair and committed suicide.

These were the bones of the legend around which Shakespeare fleshed his own King Lear, creating a passionate tragedy of filial ingratitude, and adding the dramatic sub-plot of Lear's descent into madness. Intriguingly, the inspiration for this may well have derived from an actual event involving a wealthy Kentish courtier, Sir Brian Annesley, and his three daughters, Grace, Christian and Cordell. In October 1603, Grace attempted to have her father declared insane and sent her husband to make an inventory of his chattels. Cordell, who was single and lived at home, refused to let him into the house, protesting that her father 'deserved better than at his last gasp to be registered a lunatic.' It would appear that Cordell succeeded in protecting her father, since when he died she inherited the bulk of his estate. Thus were a real-life event and old story fused together in Shakespeare's imagination and transformed into one of the greatest tragedies ever written in English literature.

THE TRIANGULAR LODGE
Gunpowder, Treason and Folly
RUSHTON, NORTHAMPTONSHIRE

As you wander the lonely backwater roads that cut through the serenely beautiful Northamptonshire countryside, you may stumble upon a curiously ostentatious building that has been described as 'the purest folly in the country.' It stands in the grounds of Rushton Hall, a late 15th-century country manor house that was once the principle estate of the Tresham family.

Ardent Catholic Sir Thomas Tresham conceived the idea for the Rushton Triangular Lodge whilst in prison for his religious beliefs. Upon his release in 1593, he set about designing a structure that would be both a clandestine declaration of his faith and a covert shrine to his suffering. The result was this remarkable three-sided, three-storeyed edifice constructed on architectural principles to commemorate the Holy Trinity and the Mass. Symbolic dates, emblems, shields, sculpted gargoyles and biblical quotations adorn the three walls, each of which has three windows, topped by three gables over which looms a three-sided chimney, festooned with Tresham trefoils.

Sir Thomas Tresham died at Rushton Hall on 11th September 1605 and was then succeeded by his 37-year-old son, Francis.

Francis was approached by his younger cousin, Robin Catesby, and asked if he would collaborate in the Gunpowder Plot.

Although it is the name of Guido Fawkes that is today most associated with the attempt by several Catholic noblemen to blow up James I and Parliament in 1605, it was Robin Catesby who conceived and led the scheme. Whether Sir Francis was ever an active plotter is debatable, but there is an unsubstantiated local tradition that the conspirators met several times at the Triangular Lodge. It has been suggested that it was Francis who unwittingly exposed the conspiracy when he wrote to his brother-in-law, Lord Monteagle, warning him to stay away from Parliament. Despite Fawkes's assertion that Tresham's role had been minor, Sir Francis was soon languishing in the Tower of London. Following his lingering death from an infection on 23rd December 1605, his body was decapitated and his head posted above the gates at the entrance of Northampton.

ABOVE: Mary Queen of Scots, cousin of Elizabeth I, was executed at Fotheringay Castle after giving her consent to a plot to assassinate the English queen.

magnet for a plethora of plots aimed at overthrowing Elizabeth. By the mid 1580s it was obvious to the queen's advisers that, as long as Mary lived, Elizabeth was in danger. It fell therefore to Sir Francis Walsingham, one of the queen's most trusted and able ministers, to provide the means by which the threat would be ended once and for all.

In December 1585 Mary and her household were moved to Chartley Hall near Stafford. Mary had found a new champion, the wealthy Catholic Anthony Babington. They had devised an ingenious method of exchanging messages: letters would be placed in watertight pouches and hidden in the bung holes of Mary's beer casks. By this means, in June 1586, Babington was able to furnish Mary with the details of his plot. Addressing her as, 'My dread Sovereign Lady and Queen,' he wrote that, 'Six noble gentlemen, all my private friends' would 'despatch the usurper' Elizabeth. He would free Mary from Chartley and then, aided by a Spanish invasion, place her upon the throne of England.

On 17th July, Mary sent her approval of the plan and, in so doing, sealed her death warrant. What neither Mary nor Babington knew was that their letters were being taken straight to Walsingham, whose clerks would copy and decipher them, before forwarding them on to their intended recipients. On 11th August 1586 Mary was arrested while hunting on the moors near Chartley. Babington and his fellow conspirators were already in custody and, under torture, had confessed everything. A search of Mary's rooms turned up masses of incriminating documents, and her fate was sealed.

She was moved to Fotheringay Castle, in the great hall of which, on 14th October 1586, her trial began. Swathed in black velvet, Mary conducted her own defence. She denied all knowledge of the Babington plot and insisted that she had not endorsed harming her cousin. However, the eloquence of her defence was far outweighed by the evidence against her and the outcome was a foregone conclusion. On 29th October, Mary Stuart was convicted and Parliament petitioned the queen that a 'just sentence might be followed by as just an execution.' Elizabeth prevaricated, however, and it wasn't until 1st February 1587 that she finally signed Mary's death warrant. At 8am on Wednesday 8th February

FOTHERINGAY CASTLE
The Execution of Mary, Queen of Scots
FOTHERINGAY, NORTHAMPTONSHIRE

Nothing now survives of Fotheringay Castle, save for a melancholic mound that overlooks a pretty and tranquil stretch of the River Nene. In summer the dense tangle of clinging vegetation that carpets its slopes is punctuated by copious Scottish thistles that are known locally as 'Queen Mary's tears', in commemoration of the fact that it was here that Mary, Queen of Scots, was executed in 1587.

On 16th May 1568, Mary, the deposed Queen of Scots, arrived in England and threw herself upon the mercy of her English cousin, Elizabeth I. For the next 19 years she would be an unwilling and unwelcome guest, held captive at a string of houses and castles. Mary's arrival threw the English court into turmoil. Not only was she next in line to Elizabeth's throne, but she was Catholic; many at home and abroad saw in her a chance to restore Catholicism to England. She became the

1587, Mary entered the great hall of Fotheringay Castle, where a crowd of around 300 people were assembled. Mounting the black draped scaffold, she told her ladies in waiting that they had 'cause rather to joy than to mourn, for now shalt thou see Mary Stuart's troubles receive their long-expected end.'

As the Scottish queen removed her gown, a murmur of disapproval rippled through the onlookers when they saw that she was wearing a scarlet petticoat, the Catholic colour of martyrdom. Blindfolded, Mary was placed upon the block, where she lay so still that the executioner was unnerved; his first blow failed to sever her head completely. 'Sweet Jesus,' she cried softly, before a second stroke finished the job. The executioner stooped to pick up the head, intending to hold it aloft with the cry 'God Save the Queen', but as his fingers gripped the mass of auburn ringlets, it was discovered that she had been wearing a wig and, to a general gasp of horror, the grey stubbly head fell to the ground and rolled across the floor. Nor did the gruesome spectacle end there. As Mary's bloodstained petticoat was being removed, something began to howl within its folds: it was the queen's lapdog, a Skye terrier. When it was finally prised away it was so caked in its mistress's blood that it proved impossible to wash it all off. The dog refused food, languished and died shortly afterwards.

Mary was interred at Peterborough Cathedral and remained there until 1612 when her son — who had succeeded Elizabeth as James I and thus united the Crowns of Scotland and England — ordered her exhumation and afforded her a royal resting place in Westminster Abbey, just a short distance from her cousin Elizabeth I.

GOTHAM
The Wise Men of Gotham
NOTTINGHAMSHIRE

Three wise men of Gotham
Went to sea in a bowl;
And if the bowl had been stronger,
My song would have been longer.

So runs a popular Victorian rhyme, but the tradition of the Wise Men of Gotham is much older, and dates back to the late medieval period. In 1540, a book entitled *The Merie Tales of the Mad Men of Gotham* was published. It contained 20 amusing anecdotes — or to be more precise, jokes with punch lines — concerning the eccentric behaviour of the residents of Gotham.

Perhaps the most famous of their escapades was their attempt to capture a cuckoo by building a fence around the bush in which it was perching.

When the bird flew off over the fence, the men lamented the fact that they hadn't built it high enough.

Another tale concerns a man of Gotham who started for market with two bushels of wheat laid in a bag across his horse's back. The man himself sat just behind the bag. When another villager told him, 'Your horse is small for so much of a load' he hoisted the bag onto his shoulders and rode the beast to market, congratulating himself that he had done 'well to share the work with it, since the horse has burden enough carrying me without having also to carry this heavy bag of wheat.' Other villagers decided to hide the church bell from a group of thieves by dropping it into a deep lake.

BELOW: The story of the Wise Men of Gotham commemorates a village of fools, whose escapades delighted readers from medieval to Victorian times.

THREE·WISE·MEN·OF·GO-
-THAM·WENT·TO·SEA·IN·
A·BOWL

ABOVE: Robin Hood is the evergreen hero representing the good outlaw battling against bad authority. His story is as pertinent today as ever it was in the past, giving him immortality and timeless appeal.

OPPOSITE: It is to the leafy glades and forest paths of Sherwood Forest that people from all over the world come in search of England's most famous outlaw – Robin Hood.

'How will we know where to find it later?' asked one. 'We'll mark the spot where we dropped it,' replied a companion and, so saying, carved a cross into the side of their boat with his dagger before rowing ashore!

According to a legend that was already old by the time *The Merie Tales* appeared in print, ingenuity rather than madness lay behind the Gothamites's bizarre antics. King John was one day intending to travel to Nottingham and pass through Gotham. It was customary for any route travelled by the king automatically to become a public highway. The villagers did not want to pay for the upkeep of a new highway and, since madness was thought to be contagious, when the king's messengers arrived, they found the inhabitants engaged in numerous acts of apparent insanity. When news of this reached the king, he quickly changed direction to avoid the village of 'mad men'.

Whatever its inspiration the book was an immediate success and became immensely popular with English royalty, nobility and churchmen. In later editions the word *Mad* was changed to *Wise* and the legend of *The Wise Men of Gotham* was born. Such was the book's enduring and universal appeal that it continued to be republished, unchanged right up to the end of the 19th century, and was even exported to America by Washington Irvine, who conferred the dubious label 'Gotham City' (a city of fools) upon his native New York.

SHERWOOD FOREST
Robin Hood: Immortal Outlaw of the Forest
NOTTINGHAMSHIRE

Robyn was a proude outlawe,
Whyles he walked on ground,
So curteyse an outlawe as he was one
Was never none y founde.

A Lytell Geste of Robyn Hode

Robin Hood is one of Britain's most famous yet most elusive figures. Two forests – Yorkshire's Barnsdale and Nottinghamshire's Sherwood – claim him as their own; roads, rivers, crags, bays, wells and pubs all over the country bear his name; and yet debate still rages over whether he ever existed and, if he did, when. He has become synonymous with medieval England, yet the ease with which successive generations of storytellers have been able to adapt him to their own age has made him timeless and kept the flame of his adventures burning for almost 700 years.

Apart from a handful of vague, and often contradictory, references in medieval records, most of what we know about Robin Hood today has evolved from a series of. popular medieval ballads. The earliest known literary reference to him appears in William Langland's *The Vision of Piers Ploughman*, published in 1377, in which Sloth – the personification of one of the Seven Deadly Sins – confesses that he is well versed in the rhymes of Robin Hood. Since Langland obviously assumes that his audience will understand the allusion without requiring an explanation, we can deduce that tales of Robin Hood, in ballad form at least, were in wide circulation by the latter half of the 14th century.

In about 1495, Wynkyn de Worde published *A Lytell Geste of Robyn Hode* ('geste' being derived from *gestsa*, Latin for story), one of the earliest collections of the then extant ballads about him. In it Robin is depicted as a 14th-century outlaw who probably lived in the reign of Edward II (1307–27). Although his abode is placed firmly in Yorkshire's Barnsdale Forest, and not Sherwood, the *Geste* does introduce the infamous villain with whom Robin's story will henceforth become intertwined, the Sheriff of Nottingham. It also features Little John, Will Scathlock (Scarlet) and Much, the miller's son, establishing the tradition of Robin's merry men.

The Robin Hood of these early ballads is far removed from the dispossessed and chivalrous nobleman of later tradition. He is a god-fearing man of his age, devoted to the Virgin Mary and fashioned to appeal to the skills, tastes, fears and aspirations of the common people. He is emphatically a yeoman, and a violent one to boot. He is skilled at archery. Although he happily, though selectively, steals from the rich, he most certainly does not give the proceeds to the poor. His enemies are dishonest officials, high churchmen and the grasping, avaricious abbots of the great monasteries, such as St Mary's in York. In the Middle Ages the church was rich, powerful and often corrupt; the great monasteries owned vast amounts of land and taxed the common people mercilessly. By depicting churchmen as the villainous victims of Robin Hood's crimes, the ballad-mongers were able to justify his criminality, whilst at the same time appeal to a deep-rooted resentment within their audiences.

As later storytellers adapted the ballads to suit different audiences and locations, Robin Hood began to soak up other legends. In 1280, the French poet and musician Adam de la Halle had written *Li Gieues de Robin et de Marion (The Game of Robin and Marion)*. The love-struck couple were pastoral sweethearts who became a popular feature of the Whitsun games in France. In England, this Robin appears to have been merged with Robin Hood, and to have been absorbed into the May Day games at

some stage in the 16th century. Marion came to represent the Queen of the May and, as Maid Marian, became an inseparable part of the Robin Hood legend. Another popular feature of the May games was the character of a drunken and dissolute clergyman who, despite having numerous different personifications, found his way into Robin's band as Friar Tuck.

As the age of the Tudors dawned, the upper classes began showing an interest in Robin Hood, and thus he evolved to suit more refined tastes. In 1598, playwright Anthony Munday

(1560–1633) wrote *The Downfall of Robert Earl of Huntingdon* and *The Death of Robert Earl of Huntingdon*, in which Robin's social standing was elevated to that of nobleman. Munday also established many of the traditions that are now an integral part of the Robin Hood legend. Firstly, he placed his fictitious earl as living in the reign of Richard I, but at a time when Richard was away on a crusade, and his brother John was ruling as regent. Secondly, Maid Marian became Matilda, daughter of Robert Fitz Walter, whom the evil Prince John desired as his mistress. Thanks to John's machinations, Robert was outlawed, and took the name Robin Hood. A series of complicated plots followed involving, amongst others, the Sheriff of Nottingham and Robert's uncle, the prior of York, before Richard's return from his crusade finally resolved everything.

Thus, by the beginning of the 17th century, the Robin Hood legend had acquired most of the ingredients to which books and, later, films and television series would adhere. It was around this time, also, that Sherwood Forest appears to have outgrown Barnsdale as his greenwood abode. The early ballads had actually mentioned both. It is probable that two different traditions, concerning two different outlaws in two different forests, were fused together as the legend of Robin Hood gained in popularity and evolved into the version that would carry his name far beyond the confines of any one locality.

And that, of course, is the important point. Robin Hood belongs to all men and to all ages. His appeal has always been his ability to adapt to new surroundings. He is the evergreen hero, the good outlaw battling the evils of bad authority. He is as much an inspiration today as ever he was in the past and, as such, Robin Hood, the champion of the people, will never die.

ago, but the Head Shrine – once the third most popular pilgrim destination in England – still survives. It is from the dizzying heights of a nearby pier that one of the cathedral's most charming features, the Lincoln Imp, keeps a watchful eye on the comings and goings of visitors below.

There is a curious legend as to how this innocuous little figure, now revered as an unofficial symbol of the city, came to be sitting on his lofty perch. In the 14th century, so one version of the story goes, Satan sent two little imps to wreak devilish mayhem upon the good citizens of Lincoln. They got off to a good start by tripping up the bishop, and then proceeded to smash all the tables and chairs in the cathedral. Finally they turned their attentions to the Angel Choir, and were in the process of defacing its stonework and monuments when an angel suddenly appeared and ordered them to desist. One of the imps fled the scene immediately, but his companion flew up to a stone pillar, and began hurling heavy stone blocks at the cherub, accompanying the assault with satanic curses and ungodly oaths. Outraged by this disrespectful behaviour, the angel responded by turning the malevolent little creature to stone and left him petrified upon this lofty roost forevermore.

LINCOLN CATHEDRAL
The Lincoln Imp
LINCOLN

Lincoln Cathedral's Angel Choir is named for the abundance of cherubic figures that adorn its stonework. It was built to cater for pilgrims who came to worship at the shrine of St Hugh, whose body was exhumed in preparation for removal to a new resting place here in 1280. Unfortunately, the holy cadaver's head somehow came off en route and the cathedral authorities, anxious to capitalize on such a heaven-sent opportunity, created two memorials to the saint, enabling pilgrims to pay homage at both the Head Shrine and the Body Shrine. The latter disappeared long

'LET ALL THE WORLD KNOW THAT THE POWER OF MONARCHS IS VAIN... NO ONE DESERVES THE NAME OF KING BUT HE WHOSE WILL THE HEAVENS, EARTH AND SEA OBEY.'

KING CANUTE BEFORE HIS FAWNING SUBJECTS

GAINSBOROUGH OLD HALL
King Canute
GAINSBOROUGH, LINCOLNSHIRE

Gainsborough Old Hall is one of the most complete medieval manor houses to survive in England today. It teeters on the edge of a tide of urban development, but remains beyond its reach, a delightful fusion of ancient stone and tasteful restoration. Although the present building was only begun between 1465 and 1485, it stands on the site of a much older castle where one of Britain's best-known apocryphal legends may have taken place.

It was at the old castle on 2nd February 1014 that King Sweyn of Denmark, ruthless leader of the great Danish invasion of England, died in torment. Rumour was rife that his death came at the avenging hands of the spear-wielding spectre of St Edmund, who had been martyred by the Danes 140 years earlier, and whose town of Bury St Edmunds Sweyn had threatened to destroy.

ABOVE: Gainsborough Old Hall is one of England's most complete medieval manor houses. It stands on the site of the old castle, which was one of the many places where King Canute is said to have attempted to order back the tide.

OPPOSITE: The Lincoln Imp gazes down from his lofty perch inside Lincoln Cathedral and has become the unofficial emblem of the city.

BELOW: King Sweyn, the Danish leader, is said to have died in torment at Gainsborough Old Castle in 1014, when the spear-wielding spectre of St Edmund appeared to him.

His devoutly Christian son, Canute, succeeded him and was duly proclaimed king at Gainsborough Castle. It was here that, having grown tired of the constant flattery heaped upon him by his eager subjects, Canute is said to have undertaken a demonstration that he hoped would dampen their belief in his god-like status. The River Trent, which flows close by, is famous for the 'aegir', a 2-metre (6-foot) high wall of water that comes rushing upriver with the spring tides. Canute had his courtiers carry his throne to the river's bank and, as the wall of water swept towards him, held up his hand and ordered it to stop. However, the aegir carried on regardless, and the worried courtiers watched as the raging torrent swept over their king. When the waves had subsided, the drenched monarch stood before his subjects and, in an unfaltering voice, told them, 'Let all the world know that the power of monarchs is vain... no one deserves the name of King but He whose Will the Heavens, Earth and Sea obey.'

LEGENDS
of WINDSWEPT MOORS and
GENTLE VALLEYS

Had I the heavens' embroidered cloths,
Enwrought with golden and silver light,
The blue and the dim and the dark cloths
Of night and light and the half light,
I would spread the cloths under your feet:
But I, being poor, have only my dreams;
I have spread my dreams under your feet;
Tread softly because you tread on my dreams.

AEDH WISHES FOR THE CLOTHS OF HEAVEN
BY WILLIAM BUTLER YEATS (1865–1939)

SHROPSHIRE, STAFFORDSHIRE, CHESHIRE & DERBYSHIRE

The counties of Shropshire, Staffordshire, Cheshire and Derbyshire offer an intriguing contrast of beautiful natural scenery and industrial landscapes. The coal, iron and other mineral deposits that were discovered and mined here helped fuel the expansion of the British Empire and have left visible scars all across the region. Many of the chimneys and kilns that once pumped pollutants into the atmosphere are today silent, yet they possess an aura of mystery and detachment that is vaguely reminiscent of that found at some of Britain's more ancient monuments. Within this industrial heartland can also be found the awesome beauty of the Peak District, where rocky crags rise from rugged moorlands and underground caverns conceal magical arrays of stalactites and stalagmites. Elsewhere gentle valleys, through which streams babble and tranquil rivers wend their way, nestle alongside the foundations of ancient structures whose origins are long forgotten. All in all it is a landscape where the myths and legends of the distant past sit side by side with the folklore of more recent events.

KEY

1. The Stiperstones
2. Boscobel House
3. Shelton
4. Mucklestone Church
5. Gawsworth Hall
6. Alderley Edge
7. Haddon Hall
8. St Mary and All Saints Church

THE STIPERSTONES
The Devil's Chair
NR STIPERSTONES, SHROPSHIRE

When you stand amongst these immense boulders that lie scattered along a rocky ridge close to the English and Welsh border, your imagination soars into the realms of exquisite fantasy. One tradition concerning their origin claims that the Devil, en route from Ireland with an apron full of stones, paused to rest and accidently dropped the boulders as he took off to continue his journey. So strong is the belief that Satan had a hand in bringing them to this windswept plateau that the largest of the stones is known as the Devil's Chair. It is said that anyone brave (or foolish) enough to spend a night in it will awake in the morning either inspired or insane!

BOSCOBEL HOUSE
Charles II and the Royal Oak
NR TONG, SHROPSHIRE

In August 1651, Charles II mustered an army of some 17,000 Scots and marched into England, determined to reclaim his throne from Cromwell's Commonwealth. On 3rd September, his force suffered a crushing defeat at the Battle of Worcester, and the young king fled the town. Cromwell offered a reward of £1,000 for Charles's capture and threatened anyone caught aiding him with the death penalty. So began six weeks of pursuit as Charles headed north, seeking shelter at loyalist safe houses along the way. His most famous adventure en route is that concerning his time spent concealed in the branches of the oak tree at Boscobel House.

Charles Giffard, whose family then owned the house, escorted the king from the battlefield and, on arrival at the family estate, summoned the five Royalist Pendrill brothers — Richard, William, George, Humphrey and John — to assist. They cut Charles's hair short, blackened his face and arms, and dressed him in the rough clothes of a woodsman to disguise his identity.

The next night, guided by Richard Pendrill, Charles set out under cover of darkness and endeavoured to cross the border into Wales, where he hoped to reach Swansea and find passage to France. The bridges and ferries over the River Severn were heavily guarded, however,

forcing their return to Boscobel House, where they were met by Colonel Carlos, the Royalist commander who had led the final charge at the Battle of Worcester. Hearing that Cromwell's soldiers had arrived in the district, it was now imperative to conceal the king and thus, as dawn was

PREVIOUS PAGES: Tradition claims that the Devil scattered the Stiperstones, when he accidently dropped a pile of boulders he was carrying to Ireland.

BELOW: If you are brave (or foolish) enough to spend the night in the rocky Stiperstones' Devil's Chair you will either be inspired or insane come break of day.

ABOVE: As Charles II tried to evade capture after his forces' defeat at the Battle of Worcester, he was forced to take refuge in the upper branches of an oak tree close to Shropshire's Boscobel House.

LEFT: Unaware that their prey is hiding above them in the oak tree, a couple of Roundhead soldiers search for the royal fugitive Charles II.

breaking – and with enemy troops searching the woods nearby – Charles and Carlos climbed into the higher branches of a huge oak tree near the house, and spent an uncomfortable day shielded from their enemies. They spent that night secreted at Boscobel House and, shortly afterwards, disguised as the servant of Jane Lane – sister of another Royalist supporter – Charles managed to reach Shoreham and escape to France, where his filthy, unkempt appearance appalled the French court.

With the Restoration of the monarchy in 1660, Charles granted numerous gifts, pensions and annuities to those who had assisted his escape. In 1664, the king's birthday, 29th May, was designated Oak Apple Day and was celebrated for over 200 years by the wearing of a sprig of oak leaves. Although the day itself is no longer celebrated, the event is still remembered in the, literally, hundred of inns and taverns that bear the title 'The Royal Oak'.

SHELTON
John Astbury and the Elers Brothers
NR HANLEY, STAFFORDSHIRE

You cannot drink tea out of a teacup without the aid of the five towns; because you cannot eat a meal in decency without the aid of the five towns. For this the architecture of the five towns is an architecture of ovens and chimneys; for this its atmosphere is as black as mud; for this it burns and smokes all night, so that Longshaw has been compared to hell.

The Old Wives' Tale
By Arnold Bennett (1867–1931)

ABOVE: Many of Stoke-on-Trent's kilns are no longer ablaze and stand as urban memorials to the glory days of Staffordshire pottery.

The 'Five Towns' of The Potteries that Arnold Bennett immortalized are, in fact, six towns, and the landscape about which he wrote has changed beyond recognition. The furnaces that blazed the names of Wedgwood, Doulton, Spode and Twyford across the globe still burn, but their brightness diminishes with each passing year and modern offices now cover the site on which John Astbury (1688–1743) perfected the glazing technique that helped launch The Potteries.

John Astbury is a largely forgotten figure in the history of Staffordshire pottery. Yet he is a legend, whose fortunes were founded on an astonishing piece of industrial espionage. In 1690 two Dutch potters, John and David Elers, arrived in nearby Bradwell and established a factory where they began manufacturing a far-superior product to that of the locals. The Elers brothers jealously guarded their techniques and came up with a rather novel method of ensuring that none of their employees could steal their ideas: they only ever employed halfwits. This lowered efficiency, but was more than compensated for by the fact that their motley workforce of imbeciles and idiots couldn't even name the day of the week, let alone memorize secret formulae and complex processes.

John Astbury, however, posed as a dullard and managed to gain employment with the unsuspecting Dutchmen, who found him so obtuse that they allowed him to work in every department of the factory. He played his role to perfection. Each duty would be explained to him over and over again, yet still he (apparently) couldn't understand. He endured many a cuff from his exasperated superiors as they endeavoured to make him comprehend, but all the time they were imprinting their industrial secrets upon his memory.

For two years John Astbury maintained the façade. Then, certain he'd learnt as much as was necessary, he feigned a malignant illness. Whilst supposedly recuperating at home he experimented with his hard-earned knowledge and formulated the plans for his future prosperity. When he returned to work, his employers were alarmed to find that the mysterious ailment had somehow improved his intelligence and promptly fired him. Soon afterwards, the imbecilic former employee opened a competing factory in Shelton, and the Elers brothers departed the district in disgust.

MUCKLESTONE CHURCH
The Battle of Blore Heath
MUCKLESTONE, STAFFORDSHIRE

On 23rd September 1459, the first major field battle of the Wars of the Roses took place. Queen Margaret of Anjou – wife of Henry VI – had ordered a Lancastrian force of some 10,000 men, led by Lord Audley, to intercept a Yorkist army of approximately 7,000, commanded by the Earl of Salisbury.

BELOW: This anvil in Mucklestone churchyard commemorates the legend that Queen Margaret of Anjou had the village blacksmith put her horse's shoes on backwards to conceal the direction of her escape.

The two sides faced each other across the Hempmill Brook on Blore Heath, with Salisbury claiming the higher ground and cunningly concealing the two wings of his militia on either side of the slope up which the Lancastrians would have to charge.

Superior in numbers, and seeing only the central body of his opposition, Lord Audley felt confident of victory and bided his time. Salisbury, on the other hand, was well aware that the queen might, at any moment, be bringing up extra forces behind him. He therefore feigned a retreat in the hope of luring his adversary into attacking. Fooled by the ruse, Audley gave the order to charge and his men waded into the brook and flung themselves up the slopes on the other side. Weighed down by their heavy armour, however, they were soon floundering in the mud. The concealed Yorkist archers loosed a volley of deadly arrows as their fleeing comrades wheeled round and plunged mercilessly into the wallowing Lancastrian ranks. Over 2,000 Lancastrians were slaughtered, including Lord Audley, and the Hempmill Brook is said to have run red with the blood of the slain for three days.

Queen Margaret reputedly watched the decimation from the church tower at Mucklestone. When it became evident that all was lost she made ready to flee and ordered the local blacksmith, William Skelhorn, to put her horse's shoes on backwards in order to obscure the route of her escape. No sooner had he performed the task than he was executed to prevent him revealing the deception. The anvil on which he is said to have worked is still preserved in front of Mucklestone Church.

GAWSWORTH HALL
Mary Fitton –
Shakespeare's Dark Lady?
GAWSWORTH, CHESHIRE

Two loves I have of comfort and despair,
Which like two spirits do suggest me still:
The better angel is a man, right fair,
The worser spirit a woman coloured ill...

Sonnet 144
By William Shakespeare (1564–1616)

When Shakespeare put quill to parchment and wrote theses opening lines, he could not have known that, almost 400 years after his death, scholars would still be arguing over the identity of his 'woman coloured ill' or, as she is better known, the 'Dark Lady' of the sonnets.

Shakespeare addressed a total of 24, apparently autobiographical, sonnets to this mystery woman with whom he evidently enjoyed a passionate affair. In an age when the paragon of feminine beauty was fair hair and pale skin, Shakespeare reveals that his 'mistress' is unfashionably dark-haired, dark-browed and dark-eyed. Furthermore he obviously considers her to be dark in spirit and totally amoral. Lines such as, 'When my love swears that she is made of truth, I do believe her, though I know she lies' do not exactly paint an endearing picture. The one thing he doesn't reveal is her identity. Numerous contenders have been put forward, including Mary Fitton (1578–1647), an intriguing lady who lived at Gawsworth Hall and is buried in the nearby parish church of St James the Great.

Around 1595, Mary Fitton became a maid of honour to Queen Elizabeth I. Sir William Knollys, comptroller of the royal household, promised her father that he would protect his 'innocent lamb' from the 'wolfish cruelty and fox-like subtlety of the tame beasts of this place.' Sir William appears to have shown more than a custodial interest in his young charge and she, by all accounts, did not discourage his attentions. In 1600, Mary also became the mistress of William Herbert, later Earl of Pembroke, by whom she became pregnant. Although their child, a son, died soon after birth, Mary was dismissed from court.

There is no proof that she also found the time to become the mistress of William Shakespeare, and the suggestion that she was indeed the 'Dark Lady' is based upon a series of tenuous claims and presumptions. Chief amongst these is that William Herbert, the Earl of Pembroke, was the 'Mr W.H.' to whom the 1609 edition of the sonnets is dedicated. That being the case, it can then be presumed that he was the 'better angel' and therefore the man who, according to the sonnets, ultimately steals Shakespeare's mistress. Many who favour Mary's claim also argue that the opening lines of sonnet 135, 'Whoever hath her wish, thou hast thy *Will*, And *Will* to boot, and *Will* in overplus', make punning reference to her three lovers: Knollys, Herbert and Shakespeare. One problem with this is that the imagery of the sonnets suggests that they may have been written in 1593, at which time William Herbert was just 13 years old. If they were written later, there is still the problem that Shakespeare states that his mistress is, like him, married, whilst Mary Fitton, at the time of her involvement with Herbert, was most certainly single. Furthermore, it would

ABOVE: Mary Fitton, a possible contender for Shakespeare's mysterious 'Dark Lady of the Sonnets', lies buried in Gawsworth Church.

appear that Mary Fitton had brown hair and grey eyes, whereas Shakespeare is emphatic that the hair colouring of the woman he is writing about is 'raven black'.

Whoever the 'Dark Lady' was, she certainly made quite an impression upon William Shakespeare, even though his feelings for her are certainly tinged with resentment, as evidenced by his parting lines:

I have sworn thee fair, and thought thee bright
Who art as black as hell, as dark as night.

ALDERLEY EDGE
The Legend of the Wizard
CHESHIRE

The legend-soaked outcrop at Alderley Edge is riddled with a series of mysterious caverns that were first hewn from the sandstone by Bronze Age men. It is a chilling, yet mellow, place. Crows wheel in and out of crumbling crevices, their raucous cries carried upon faint breezes, sending shivers of nervous anticipation down the spines of visitors. From one mossy rock face a steady dribble of water drips into a tiny trough, above which you can just about discern the weathered face of a bearded man and the invitation: 'Drink of this and take thy fill, for the water falls by the wizard's will.' Some claim that the wizard depicted here is Merlin and that, deep within the rock, King Arthur and a retinue of knights still sleep in enchanted repose.

Long ago a farmer from nearby Mobberley was riding his milk-white mare over Alderley Edge on his way to Macclesfield Fair. He intended to sell the beast that day, and let the horse set its own pace so that it would arrive fresh at market and fetch a high price. As he came close to the spot known as 'Thieves' Hole', his mount suddenly stopped and, moments later, there appeared on the path before them an old man with long white hair and beard. He offered the farmer a sum of money for the mare, but the man declined, convinced he could get a much better price at market. 'Go then,' chided the old man, 'but mark my words, none will buy and I shall meet you here at sunset to conclude our business.' The farmer laughed and, bidding the stranger, 'Good day', spurred his horse on for the fair.

To his great surprise, nobody would buy the mare, and it was with an air of disappointment that the farmer rode back over Alderley Edge that night. The old man was awaiting his arrival, and led him to a great slab of rock embedded in the hillside. He lightly tapped the rock with his staff whereupon it split in two, revealing a pair of heavy iron gates that opened slowly with a sound like thunder. The farmer fell to the ground and begged the wizard to spare his life. 'Fear nothing,' came the reply, 'just follow and behold a sight which no mortal eye has ever seen.' So saying the old man stepped through the gates and, nervously, the farmer followed.

They went through a succession of caverns, passing countless numbers of slumbering knights. By the side of all but one there slept a milk-white horse. 'Their numbers are not complete,' said the old man, 'your horse is needed to make them so.' As he said this they entered another cavern where piles of gold, silver and precious stones were heaped on the ground.

RIGHT: The twisted trees around Alderley Edge lend the area a strange aura and hide a possible resting place of King Arthur and his knights.

'**HERE THEY LIE IN AN ENCHANTED SLEEP AWAITING THE DAY WHEN ENGLAND IS IN PERIL. THENCE SHALL THEY DESCEND INTO THE PLAIN TO DECIDE THE FATE OF A GREAT BATTLE AND SAVE THEIR COUNTRY.'**

MERLIN SPEAKS TO THE FARMER AT ALDERLEY EDGE

The wizard told him to take as much as he could carry as payment for the horse. It was a wealthy man whom the wizard led back past the sleeping knights, pausing to explain that, 'Here they lie in an enchanted sleep awaiting the day when England is in peril. Thence shall they descend into the plain to decide the fate of a great battle and save their country.'

Moments later the farmer found himself alone on Alderley Edge. In the years that followed he often returned to search for the entrance to the cave, but always without success. No mortal since has ever gazed upon the sleeping knights or seen the vast treasures that the farmer swore to his dying day lie deep beneath Alderley Edge.

HADDON HALL
The Legend of Dorothy Vernon
NR BAKEWELL, DERBYSHIRE

Beautifully situated atop a limestone outcrop and overlooking a picturesque reach of the River Wye, Haddon Hall — with its lofty battlements and towering turrets — is one of the most peaceful and elegant buildings in England. Arrive here on an early autumn morning, when it floats upon a carpet of white mist, and you feel that you've stumbled into a fairy-tale realm.

The most famous of Haddon Hall's stories is that of Dorothy Vernon whose father, Sir George, was renowned for his heavy-handed discipline. He took an instant dislike to Sir John Manners, a determined suitor with whom Dorothy was enamoured. He forbade his daughter to have anything to do with him, and encouraged her elder sister, Margaret, to keep a watchful eye over her sibling to ensure that she did not disobey him.

BELOW: On autumn mornings, Haddon Hall often floats above a carpet of mist, giving the distinct impression you've arrived in a fairy-tale realm.

On the day of Margaret's marriage, Dorothy and Sir John hatched a plan to elope. As the guests were celebrating in the Long Gallery, Dorothy slipped quietly away. She moved quickly down the steps, through the gardens, and over the small packhorse bridge where her lover was waiting, disguised as a woodsman. Together the eager couple rode through the night, and next day were married at Aylestone in Leicestershire. Sir George eventually accepted their marriage, and, when he died in 1567, the hall and estate passed to Dorothy. Thus ended several hundred years of tenure by the Vernons, and ownership passed to the Manners family, whose descendent, the Duke of Rutland, still owns it today.

ST MARY AND ALL SAINTS CHURCH
The Twisted Spire
CHESTERFIELD, DERBYSHIRE

The cathedral-sized parish church of St Mary and All Saints testifies to the importance of Chesterfield in the 13th and 14th centuries. The bizarre spire that surmounts it is an eye-catching landmark around whose twisted fabric swirl tales of demonic dabbling and impish intrigue. Unskilled craftsmen using unseasoned timber during the Black Death of 1348 were probably responsible for the distortion. Where a structural surveyor might detect the careless hand of a bungling builder, legend has thrown caution to the wind and declared the impediment as the work of the Devil.

One tale tells how the Devil, en route for Derby, paused to rest on St Mary's spire as a wedding was taking place in the church below. As the couple left the church, he was so surprised to hear that the bride was a virgin that he turned round to look at her and, in his astonishment, bent the spire. Another account blames the twist on the Devil getting his tail caught around the spire as he was flying over the church.

RIGHT: Legend holds that it was the Devil's work rather than poor craftsmanship that gave Chesterfield's Church of St Mary and All Saints its distinctively twisted spire.

A third tradition holds that two imps, whom Satan had sent to unleash mayhem and destruction on Lincoln Cathedral, paused at Chesterfield. They sat upon the church spire and began mischievously twisting it into the corkscrew that we see today.

Mysterious Land where Merlin Sleeps

When I remember all
The friends, so link'd together,
I've seen around me fall
Like leaves in wintry weather;
I feel like one
Who treads alone
Some banquet-hall deserted,
Whose lights are fled,
Whose garlands dead,
And all but he departed!
Thus, in the stilly night,
Ere slumber's chain has bound me.
Sad Memory brings the light
Of other days around me.

From *The Light of Other Days*
Thomas Moore (1779–1852)

WALES

The ancestors of the Welsh people were actually ancient Britons, driven westwards by Saxon invaders who, unable to understand the language of those whose lands they had taken, called them 'Welsh', meaning 'foreigner'. As these vanquished people settled into their mountain fastness, they dreamt of the day when they would be able to return to reclaim their land. They called themselves *Cymry*, meaning 'comrades', and named their mountainous domain *Cymru*, meaning 'for their land'. Their hopes and dreams were kept alive by bards and storytellers. Most important of all was the knowledge that Arthur lay sleeping at a secret location, awaiting the day when he would ride forth to lead his countrymen to victory and, just as Merlin had predicted, place one of their own upon the throne of England.

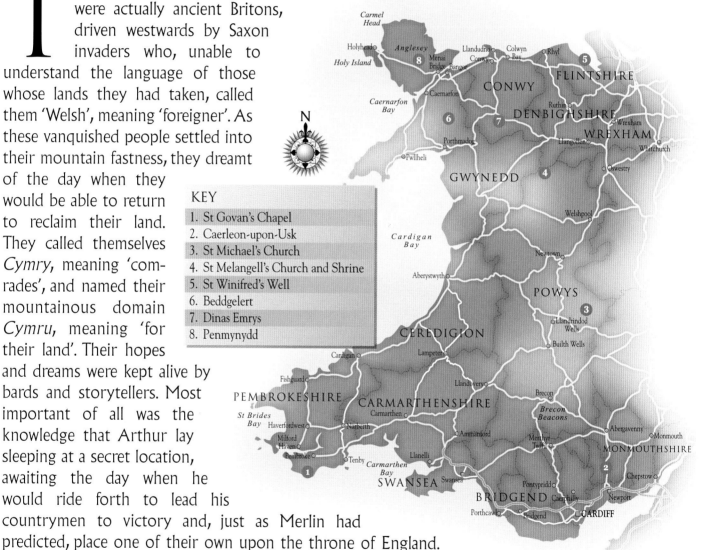

KEY
1. St Govan's Chapel
2. Caerleon-upon-Usk
3. St Michael's Church
4. St Melangell's Church and Shrine
5. St Winifred's Well
6. Beddgelert
7. Dinas Emrys
8. Penmynydd

ST GOVAN'S CHAPEL
The Saint and the Pirates
NR BUSHERTON, PEMBROKESHIRE

Despite the unholy proximity of a military firing range, St Govan's Chapel is a truly spiritual place where legend and nature combine to create a sea-sprayed haven of magic and mystery. Historically, St Govan – whose real name was

Gobham or Gobban – is said to have lived in the 6th century and is thought to have been the abbot of a monastery at Dairinis in Wexford, Ireland. One day he was sailing along the Pembrokeshire coast when pirates attacked his vessel. With the scurvy brigands in hot pursuit, Gobham headed for the coast. A fissure suddenly opened to allow him to pass into the cliff, and then closed behind him until danger had passed. Gobham was overcome by guilt at his cowardice and vowed to spend

the rest of his days as a hermit. He duly built a cell at the spot where divine intervention had thwarted the pirates' ambitions. The holy hermit saw out his days at this rugged location and, when he died, was buried beneath the stone altar around which his followers built the secluded little chapel. Parts of the building seen today may well date back to the 6th century, although most of it was built in the 11th century.

The moment you begin the precarious descent down the time-worn steps leading to the chapel you are walking on legend, for tradition asserts that no mortal can ever count the number of steps accurately. Certainly the tally on the ascent rarely corresponds with that of the descent, although cynics might argue that the reason lies with the irregular pattern of the steps. Behind the chapel's ancient stone altar there is a tiny cell, the rock of which bears a series of rib-like features said to be the imprint left by Gobham's body as he lay hidden from the pirates. It is also claimed that those who make a wish as they enter this fissure will find it granted if they are able to turn around inside it. Amongst the immense boulders that litter the cove below the chapel is a large stone known as the 'Bell Rock'. It is said that Gobham was given a silver bell that was stolen by pirates. The saint prayed for its return, whereupon the angels retrieved it and secured it safely inside this large boulder. Whenever Gobham tapped the rock it would give out a clear note, which sounded 1,000 times louder than the original bell.

Caerleon-upon-Usk
Arthur's Round Table
NR NEWPORT, GWENT

The town of Caerleon-upon-Usk boasts a more ancient pedigree than a cursory glance might suggest, and its origins stretch back into the mists of time. The Romans built an imposing fortress here in AD75 and named it *Isca* after the nearby river. It became the headquarters of the 2nd Augustan Legion, incorporating many of the amenities that a Roman soldier might expect to find in even the most far-flung reach of the empire. These included an amphitheatre of such daunting dimensions that later ages would bestow upon it a legendary status.

With the departure of the Romans, hard facts become sparse. Certainly the town had by then acquired its current name of Caerleon, which means simply 'City of the Legions'.

noble river [Usk] whereby the Kings and Princes that should come from overseas might be born thither in their ships, and on the other side, girdled about with meadows and woods, passing fair was the magnificence of the kingly palaces thereof with the gilded verges of the roofs that imitated Rome.

Geoffrey sparked a tourist invasion that would last for centuries and bring large numbers of people flocking to Caerleon to absorb its Arthurian spirit. The locals were only too pleased to oblige the trade and thus it was that the Roman amphitheatre, the remains of which had lain buried beneath an imposing grass mound for centuries, was soon incorporated into the legend. It was, so eager visitors were informed, the original Round Table of King Arthur.

ST MICHAEL'S CHURCH
The Dragon's Lair
CASCOB, POWYS

This peaceful church, dating largely from the 13th century, nestles peacefully amid picturesque countryside, bursting with ancient memories and legends. It is one of several churches encircling Radnor Forest that are dedicated to St Michael, the angel who, according to the *Book of Revelations*, battled with the evil dragon when there was war in heaven. Early Christians, seeking to personify the forces of good and evil, often dedicated hilltop churches to St Michael because they believed a foundation so sited would be well positioned for dealing with the forces of evil, which they knew surrounded them.

That the powers of darkness were, apparently, still active here until relatively recently is illustrated by a curious framed parchment inside the church, which bears an 'abracadabra' charm. Beneath the spell can be read the incantation that was used in the 1700s to release a local girl, Elizabeth Loyd, from 'Witchcraft' and 'all Evil spirites and all evil men or women or Wizardes.' The parishioners were so afraid of repercussions that, as further protection, they buried the charm in the churchyard where it lay undiscovered for 200 years.

It is the weather vane atop the church tower, depicting a fearsome winged dragon, that commemorates a far more ancient evil said to lurk amidst the lush woodlands of the Radnor Forest. Legend holds that the last dragon in Wales sleeps imprisoned within its sylvan expanse, its escape prevented only by the power of the ring of churches

ABOVE: The last dragon in Wales is said to sleep in Radnor Forest and is held there by a ring of churches, all of which are dedicated to St Michael, including this one at Cascob.

Doubtless much of the stone was carted off by opportunist masons and incorporated into other buildings, but a stronghold as colossal as this could not be allowed to fade away, and thus, by the 12th century, tradition had established that by the time the Romans abandoned the City of Legions it had become the royal seat of King Arthur.

It was Geoffrey of Monmouth in his *History of the Kings of Britain* (c1136) that helped place Caerleon firmly on the map: as far as he was concerned it was the site of King Arthur's coronation. By setting this momentous event at Caerleon and making it the place where the legendary monarch held court, he conferred a mystical romance upon the town. Caerleon, he says, was:

Situated in pleasant position…abounding in wealth above all other cities…on one side there flowed the

ABOVE: St Melangell's Church stands in one of the most tranquil settings in Wales, and contains northern Europe's oldest Romanesque shrine to the patron saint of hares.

dedicated to St Michael. Many believe that should one of these churches be demolished, the spell will be broken and the dragon released onto the neighbourhood.

St Melangell's Church and Shrine
The Patron Saint of Hares
NR LLANGYNOG, POWYS

Amid the peaceful tranquillity of the Berwyn Hills, where babbling streams give rise to the River Tanat, stands a remote and tiny church. It is dedicated to a little-known saint whose mortal remains are reputed to rest there.

St Melangell is thought to have been an Irish princess who fled from her father's court when he attempted to force her to marry, rather than allow her to follow her true vocation and dedicate herself to God. She arrived at this enchanting spot and remained here in holy seclusion for 15 years.

One day Brochwel, Prince of Powys, was hunting in the more remote reaches of the forest when his hounds started a hare and pursued the terrified creature into a secluded grove. As they moved in for the kill, they froze and stood rooted to the spot. The huntsman raised his horn to blow a blast of encouragement, but it stuck to his lips and would not sound a note. The bemused prince barged into the brush and found St Melangell kneeling at prayer with the hare nestling safely amongst the folds of her robes. The prince asked how she came to be residing in his forest, and was so moved by her story that he made her a gift of the land upon which they were standing as a perpetual refuge and place of sanctuary.

Thus St Melangell became the patron saint of hares, and her church the place of holy pilgrimage that it remains today. The tale of her legendary meeting with Prince Brochwel is depicted on a series of winsome carvings inside the church. The vestiges of the saintly lady are said to repose within the 12th-century reliquary situated behind the main altar, which is reputed to be northern Europe's oldest Romanesque shrine.

ABOVE: When a lustful Welsh chieftain cut off St Winifred's head, it came to rest at the site where the tranquil shrine dedicated to her now stands in Holywell.

BELOW: Among those who came to St Winifred's Well were James II and his wife Mary of Modena. Their prayers were answered and they were blessed with a son.

St Winifred's Well
St Beuno's Miracle
HOLYWELL, FLINTSHIRE

St Winifred's shrine is considered the finest surviving example of a medieval holy well in Britain. Its origins are said to date from the 7th century when Winifrid (or Gwenffrwd to use her actual name), a well-connected and noble young lady, was visited by a local chieftain named Caradoc. Smitten by her beauty, the lustful chieftain attempted to seduce the saintly Gwenffrwd. When she rejected his advances he flew into a violent rage and attempted to force himself upon her. Girding up her skirts, Gwenffrwd dodged past him and ran towards a nearby chapel, where her uncle St Beuno was preaching. Caradoc caught up with her, however, and, drawing his sword, cleaved Gwenffrwd's head clean off. Justice fell swiftly upon the maiden-slaying maniac, however;

there came a great roar from beneath the ground, and the earth opened up and swallowed him. Gwenffrwd's head continued rolling down the hill, and where it finally came to rest, a spring gushed forth. Alerted by the commotion, St Beuno picked up the head and replaced it on his neice's shoulders, so restoring her to life.

By 1155, her shrine had become an important place of pilgrimage. Richard I came here to pray for his crusade. So did Henry V, both before and after his victory at Agincourt. Henry Tudor prayed at the shrine before setting out to meet Richard III at the Battle of Bosworth. James II, desperate for a male heir, brought his queen, Mary of Modena, here in 1686. His prayers were answered two years later, though not quite as he had anticipated. The birth of their son, who would become the 'Old Pretender', resulted in James losing his crown, since the British Constitution forbade a Catholic heir to the throne.

ABOVE: Many visitors shed a tear at Gelert's Grave, where Llewelyn's faithful hound reputedly lies buried, unaware that the story is an 18th-century fiction.

Even today pilgrims continue to make the journey to this tranquil and sacred spot. Sadly, however, the spring that for centuries gushed forth at an unfaltering 13,500 litres (3,000 gallons) per minute was interrupted by local mining operations, in 1917. The unfortunate situation was resolved, although the bubbling spring that visitors see today is actually fed by a concealed pipe connected to Holywell's municipal water supply!

BEDDGELERT
Gelert's Grave
GWYNEDD

One of the most poignant sites in Wales is the railed-in tomb of Gelert, the faithful hound of Llewelyn the Great. The dog was a gift to the prince from his father-in-law, King John. It proved to be a great hunter whose prowess was legendary.

One day Gelert refused to accompany his master to the hunt. So Llewelyn went alone, leaving his adored hound to guard his infant son, who was asleep in his cradle. When the prince returned, the dog came bounding to the door to greet him. Llewelyn saw that Gelert's coat was covered in blood and, rushing inside, found his son's cradle overturned and a pool of blood alongside it. Assuming that the dog had killed the child, the angry chieftain promptly drew his sword and plunged it deep into Gelert's body, killing him instantly. No sooner had he done so than there came a low murmur from beneath the upturned cot; lifting it, Llewelyn found the boy alive and well, but lying beside the mangled carcase of a wolf. Too late the anguished chieftain realized that, far from harming the boy, Gelert had saved his life.

Tearfully, Llewelyn laid his faithful hound beneath the scenic splendour of Snowdonia and, ever since, thousands of visitors have journeyed to this rural paradise to shed silent tears upon his grave. It is almost a shame to dab the tissue of truth across the legend, but David Pritchard, an enterprising 18th-century proprietor of the village inn, invented the story to attract custom and erected Gelert's Grave in a nearby field to give visitors something upon which to focus their grief.

ABOVE: It was atop Dinas Emrys in Gwynedd that Merlin made his first appearance as a boy wizard and predicted the coming of Arthur as king.

LEFT: The red dragon of Wales and the white dragon of the Saxons fought constantly with each other; Merlin prophesied that the red dragon would one day be victorious.

DINAS EMRYS
Merlin
NR BEDDGELERT, GWYNEDD

It is on the domed summit of Wales's most famous Dark Age site that we get our first tantalizing glimpse of one of the most enigmatic figures ever to stride across Britain's legendary landscape. For it is upon these rugged slopes that the youthful Merlin is said to have made his first mystical appearance as a precocious boy wizard.

The story begins with the tyrannical usurper Vortigern who, having lost his kingdom to the Saxons, took the advice of his magicians and headed for Wales in search of a suitable location to establish a citadel where he could be safe from his enemies. His wise men told him he should construct a fortress on this remote summit and his masons duly set to work, but each night, when the workers had downed tools, their construction would mysteriously disappear and, sensing evil afoot, Vortigern summoned his magicians to demand an explanation. They were mystified as to the cause of the phenomenon but the solution, they informed him, was to sacrifice a boy who had been born without a human father, and sprinkle his blood about the foundations of the building.

Messengers were duly sent to find such a boy and, in the streets of Carmarthen, they found a youth being taunted by another because he had never had a father. The boy's name was Myrddin Emrys – the future Merlin of King Arthur's court – and when he and his mother appeared before Vortigern she told the king that she knew of no man who was the boy's father. All she could tell him was that something had appeared to her in the shape of a handsome young man, embraced her, then vanished. Later she bore a child whose father was certainly not human. Vortigern was at first suspicious of the claim, but when he sought the opinion of his Druids, they told him that she had probably been the victim of an incubus – a male demon, which it was believed could ravish sleeping women.

Myrddin then demanded to know why he and his mother had been brought before Vortigern. When the king told him the reason, the boy denounced the magicians, claiming that the towers had collapsed because two dragons, one white, one red, lived in a pool beneath the hill. Each night they would awake and fight so ferociously that they caused the walls of the citadel to collapse. The masons dug deep into the hill and, just as Myrddin had predicted, discovered a pool, in the depths of which lay two sleeping dragons. The red dragon, Myrddin told the court, represented the Britons, and the white one the Saxons. They would continue to fight for many generations until eventually the red dragon would be victorious and would drive the white one away.

Myrddin went into a trance and foretold of a sequence of calamitous events. The sons of King Constantine – whose murder Vortigern had instigated and whose throne he had usurped – were at that very moment preparing an invasion. They would, he continued, defeat the accursed Saxons, but before that 'they will besiege you [Vortigern] in a tower and set fire to it.' He continued to say that the elder brother, Aurelius Ambrosius, would be crowned king but would die from poisoning. His younger brother Uther Pendragon would succeed him, but his reign too, would be cut short by poison leaving his son, Arthur, to inherit the throne and avenge his father's death.

So it was that Merlin made his first prediction of the coming of the king whose conception he would ultimately facilitate (see page 17), and thus it was that the red dragon became the symbol of Wales.

PENMYNYDD
The Birthplace of Owen Tudor
ISLE OF ANGLESEY

Just before the road from Llangefni climbs into Penmynydd, a rough track heads off through the lush countryside and passes a remote huddle of farm buildings surrounding a sturdy house, where began the fulfilment of Merlin's prophecy that one day a Welshman would sit upon the throne of England. Today there is nothing about this anonymous mass of old and new stone to suggest that, 500 years ago, the seed of modern Britain was sown here with the birth of Owen Tudor, father of the Tudor dynasty.

When Henry V died suddenly in 1422, he left behind a beautiful widow, Katherine of Valois, and a baby son whose reign as Henry VI would witness the most acute phase of the Wars of the Roses. Owen Tudor, who had shown gallant service at the Battle of Agincourt, had been made a squire of the royal bodyguard and, in the months that followed Henry's death, attended Katherine at Windsor Castle. There is a story that one day, whilst on guard duty, he was asked to dance for the queen and, determined to make a good impression, he attempted an over-ambitious pirouette and fell heavily into Katherine's lap! The manner with which she excused his *faux pas* did not go

ABOVE: When Henry Tudor defeated Richard III at the Battle of Bosworth he fulfilled Merlin's prophecy that one day a Welsh Challenger would usurp the throne of England.

unnoticed by her ladies-inwaiting. They are said to have rebuked her, pointing out that she 'lowered herself by paying any attention to a person [that] belonged to a barbarous clan of savages, reckoned inferior to the lowest English yeoman.' Katherine claimed that, being French, she was unaware of 'any difference in race in the British island.' It was evident, however, that the young queen was enamoured of the 37-year-old Welshman and, soon afterwards, the two became lovers.

By the sixth year of her son's reign, his guardians became worried by the prospect of Katherine's remarrying.

'THAT HEAD SHALL LIE ON THE STOCK THAT WAS WONT TO LIE ON QUEEN KATHARINE'S LAP.'

OWEN TUDOR'S LAST WORDS BEFORE
HE WAS BEHEADED

They passed a law threatening dire consequences for any man who dared 'marry a queen dowager, or any lady who held lands of the Crown, without the consent of the King and his council', but Owen and Katherine had already married in secret. How they managed to keep their intrigue hidden is one of the great mysteries of English history, but keep it hidden they did and she bore him several sons.

In the summer of 1436 Katherine gave birth to a baby daughter who died after only two days. The loss, coupled with the strain of her secret marriage, proved too much for her constitution. She fell ill and entered Bermondsey Abbey to be nursed. Meanwhile, news of the marriage leaked out and Owen Tudor was confined to Newgate prison whilst their sons were placed under the care of Katherine de la Pole, the Abbess of Barking.

The queen died in February 1437 and was buried in Westminster Abbey. Later that year Owen Tudor escaped and went to ground. King Henry VI issued a summons ordering that he 'the which dwelled with his mother, should come into his presence', but Owen Tudor remained in hiding. Then one day, learning that the king was being influenced by evil gossip, he suddenly appeared before the privy council, and defended himself with such verbal dexterity that Henry set him free.

Years later, in the general euphoria that followed the birth of a son to Henry and his wife, Margaret of Anjou, Owen Tudor was summoned to London, granted an annuity of £40 and made 'keeper of our parks in Denbigh Wales.' Furthermore, his sons were declared legitimate and accepted into the ranks of the nobility. Edmund was created Earl of Richmond and, through the influence of his half-brother, King

ABOVE: It was at Pembroke Castle that Henry Tudor was born. He was destined to defeat Richard III at Bosworth Field and, as Henry VII, fulfil Merlin's prophecy that one day a Welshman would sit upon the English throne.

Henry VI, married Margaret Beaufort, the 13-year-old heiress to the house of Somerset. On 26th June 1457, she gave birth to a son at Pembroke Castle. That boy, grandson of Owen Tudor and Katherine of Valois, was destined to ascend the throne of England as King Henry VII.

In 1461, at the age of 76, Owen Tudor was captured after having fought against the Yorkist forces at the battle of Mortimer's Cross. He was beheaded in Hereford market and his final words are said to have been 'That head shall lie on the stock that was wont to lie on Queen Katharine's lap.'

HEROES, HEROINES, SAINTS, GODS and HIDDEN REALMS

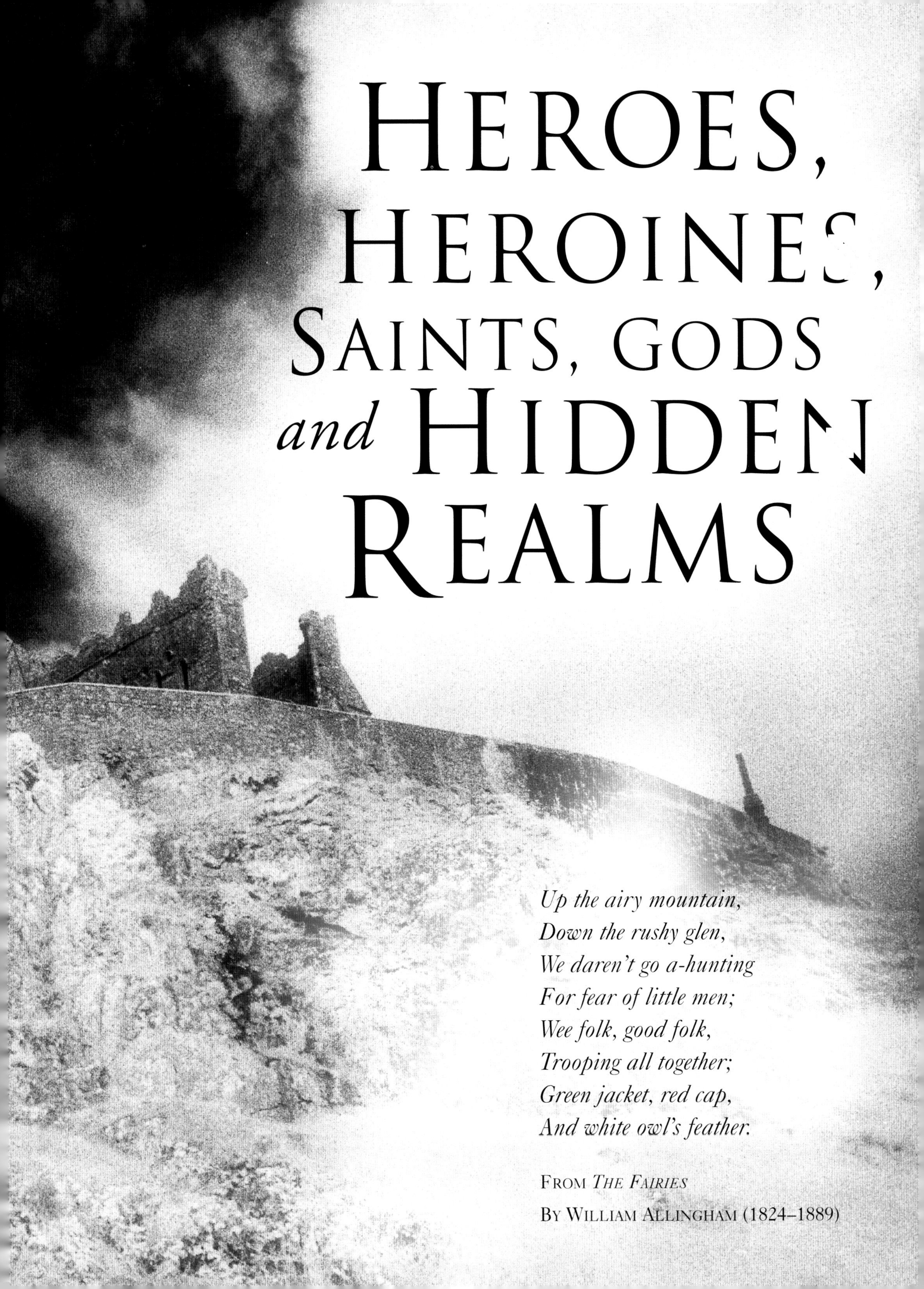

Up the airy mountain,
Down the rushy glen,
We daren't go a-hunting
For fear of little men;
Wee folk, good folk,
Trooping all together;
Green jacket, red cap,
And white owl's feather.

FROM *THE FAIRIES*
BY WILLIAM ALLINGHAM (1824–1889)

IRELAND

Although folklore maintains that five specific groups of invaders have populated Ireland, it is the penultimate of these, the Tuatha De Danann (the People of the Goddess Danu), with whom Irish myth and legend is most concerned. Having ruled the land for nine generations, this race of gods was driven out by the Milesians, from whom the present-day Irish people are said to be descended. When the De Danann queen, Eriu, was fatally wounded in battle, she made the Milesian leader, Amorgen, promise that the island would bear her name forever, and thus it became Eriu, Eire or Eireann. The Tuatha De Danann, however, did not leave Ireland but used their magical powers to retreat into a mystical realm, where they dwelt beyond the *sidhes*, those grassy mounds and barrows that speckle the landscape and are still feared today. They became the *Aes Sidhe*, or 'People of the Hills' — the fairies, whose existence is an integral part of the Irish psyche. Thus Ireland's magical history is preserved in the country's legends, and the Gaelic gift for storytelling has ensured their continued survival.

KEY

1. Ross Castle
2. Lough Gur
3. The Rock of Cashel
4. The Rath of Mullaghmast
5. The Hill of Tara
6. Lough Derravaragh
7. Rockfleet Castle
8. Antrim Castle Gardens
9. The Giant's Causeway

ROSS CASTLE
The Good O'Donoghue
KILLARNEY, COUNTY KERRY

Ross Castle sits on the tranquil shores of Lough Leane, its ghostly image rippling in the silent waters reflecting past eras of grandeur and mystery. It was once the abode of O'Donoghue Mor, a great chieftain who was, unusually for his age, as renowned for his pacific virtues as for his warring exploits. He was also considered to be one of the wisest men of his time, famed for his knowledge of the black arts.

O'Donoghue had an almost pathological fear of growing old, and one day locked himself away in the grand vaulted chamber at the top of the castle, vowing not to emerge until he had found a way of regaining his youth. Seven weeks passed. Then he called his wife to his chamber, and informed her that he had found a solution. 'You must,' he told her, 'chop me up into little pieces, put those pieces into a tub, lock that tub in this very chamber for another seven weeks and, when you next unlock the door, you will find me a child once more.' Before entrusting himself to her blade he told her that he must test her resolve by reading aloud from his black book. 'Many horrors will be conjured up,' he informed her, 'but if

ABOVE: The Lakes of Killarney are magical and mysterious, and justly famed for their tranquil beauty. Many a myth lurks in County Kerry's undulating countryside.

PREVIOUS PAGES: Once the seat of the High Kings of Munster, the Rock of Cashel was where St Patrick baptized King Aengus, and is now one of Ireland's most sacred sites.

you cry out at the sight of just one of them, then I shall be taken from you forever.' He began to read. The poor woman watched in terror as serpents and dragons reared up and lunged towards her; legions of demons spat showers of blue flame; sword-wielding giants that would test the mettle of the boldest warriors made as though to decapitate her. Through it all, not one sound did the lady utter. Even the castle shook to its foundations with an unearthly rumble, not a word passed her lips. When her own child appeared dead on the table before her, however,

> **'MANY HORRORS WILL BE CONJURED UP, BUT IF YOU CRY OUT AT THE SIGHT OF JUST ONE OF THEM, THEN I SHALL BE TAKEN FROM YOU FOREVER.'**
>
> O'DONOGHUE MOR TO HIS WIFE

lake's eastern shore becoming agitated, though the rest of the surface will remain smooth. Then a foaming wave will rush across the lough, and in its wake will come a majestic warrior in burnished armour upon a milk-white steed. He will be followed by a cavalcade of maidens and youths, linked by delightful garlands of spring flowers, their movements timed to the strains of an enchanted melody. As the cavalcade reaches the western shore of the lough, it will be gradually enveloped by early morning mists and will fade slowly away before the spellbound onlookers who, just as the last harmonious tones give way to silence, will awake, as if from a dream.

LOUGH GUR
The Sacred Lough
NR HOLYCROSS, COUNTY LIMERICK

Cradled by the protective embrace of a circle of low-lying hills, Lough Gur has long been regarded as a sacred otherworld, the haunted preserve of fairies, gods and legendary heroes. 'Lough Gur is enchanted,' wrote David Fitzgerald, in his 1879 *Popular Tales of Ireland,* 'in the past, no minstrel, piper, or poet would willingly spend a night within a mile of its shore, such was its fearful reputation and potency. Even to fall asleep in daytime on its banks was considered among them to be reckless folly.'

Tradition places Lough Gur under the aegis of Aine, the fairy love-goddess who was believed to tempt mortals into acts of passion. Maurice Fitzgerald, the first Earl of Desmond, is said to have one day encountered her as she bathed in the lough's ice-cool waters. Having taken her cloak, an action that magically placed her under his power, he was able to lie with her and from their union was born an enchanted son, Geroid Iarla. Although Maurice raised Geroid at his castle, Aine warned him that if he ever showed surprise at anything their son did, the boy would be compelled to return to her world.

As a young man Geroid showed great promise in the art of poetry and is said to have been able to compose 'witty and ingenious' verses in Gaelic. He also excelled in magic, as befitting one who was half god. One day, during a banquet at his

ABOVE: Time was when no minstrel, piper or poet would dare fall asleep on the banks of Lough Gur, which was regarded as a sacred otherworld.

she let out a shriek of anguish. A great storm suddenly erupted. Raging winds hurled themselves at the walls, howling through the nooks and crevices of the castle, whilst thunder shook the building. Suddenly, O'Donoghue was swept up in a vortex and sucked through the chamber window and into the raging waters of Lough Leane.

The memory of O'Donoghue has ever since been cherished by successive generations, and it is said that he lives in a great palace at the bottom of the lake. Every seven years, at dawn on May Day morning (the anniversary of his departure), he returns to visit his ancient domains. Those who venture here in the hope of seeing him will notice the waters around the father's castle, Geroid became involved in a competition of magical prowess with a young woman. Determined to surpass her skills, Geroid leapt in and out of a tiny bottle. On seeing his son perform such an impossible feat, Maurice let out a cry of impressed astonishment. Suddenly a cold breeze blew through the hall. Geroid left the feast and walked slowly to the shores of the lake. Turning to wave farewell to his father, he went into its waters and, as he did so, was transformed into a goose. His heartbroken father watched as the bird slowly faded away.

When the waters of Lough Gur are tranquil and still, it is said that Geroid Iarla's enchanted castle is occasionally glimpsed deep beneath the surface. Here he lives waiting for the day when he can return to the world of mortals.

Lough Gur is a special place that has been sacred to those who dwell upon its magical shores since long before Christianity came to Ireland. The rich abundance of well-preserved cromlechs, dolmens, tumuli and other archaeological treasures scattered about its shores and the surrounding countryside bear proud testimony to its mystical past. To go there in the silence of an early morning, when the sun's first rays sparkle upon its glassy surface, and the breezes are heavy with the fresh scent of the new day, it is easy to feel that the gods still walk among us.

ABOVE: A cathedral now stands on the Rock of Cashel, long considered one of Ireland's holiest places, yet the rock was said to have been planted by the Devil.

THE ROCK OF CASHEL
St Patrick and the Baptism of King Aengus
COUNTY TIPPERARY

Once the seat of the High Kings of Munster, and now one of Ireland's most sacred relics, the Rock of Cashel sits at the heart of the picturesque plain of Tipperary and boasts a venerable antiquity that stretches far back into the foggy mists of time. Strange, then, that this most hallowed of holy places should have been planted by the Devil. Tradition says that one

day the Devil was pursuing an enemy when, overcome by hunger, he paused to take a savage bite from one of the northern hills. Resuming the chase, he spat the rocky segment at his foe and so formed the Rock of Cashel. If you look towards the Slieve Bloom mountains today, you can see a gap, still known as 'Devil's Bit', into which Cashel would fit exactly.

Wandering amongst the sombre grey remnants of the ancient cathedral that sprawl across the lofty summit you come upon the replica of St Patrick's Cross, the base of which, it has long been purported, was once the inauguration stone for the Kings of Cashel. Although this is highly improbable, legend claims it as the place where St Patrick baptized

King Aengus in AD448. It was 16 years after beginning his mission in Ireland that the elderly and decidedly feeble St Patrick finally reached the Rock of Cashel. As he prepared to administer the sacrament of baptism, he felt a little unsteady and drove the spiked point of his crozier firmly into the ground for support.

When the ceremony was over, the onlookers noticed that the grass was soaked in blood and, looking down, St Patrick saw that he had inadvertently driven the sharp tip of his crozier through Aengus's foot. Apologizing, the saint asked the king why he had not cried out in pain, to which the king replied that he had heard so much about the sufferings of Jesus that he would have proudly endured the agony, even had he not believed that it was part of the ceremony!

THE RATH OF MULLAGHMAST
The Wizard Earl
NR BALLITORE, COUNTY KILDARE

The tranquil air of mystery that surrounds this ancient ring fort belies a stormy and violent past. There is plenty of evidence to suggest that many a vicious battle was fought upon its slopes in the 2nd and 3rd centuries. The most notorious act of brutal infamy to taint the magic of this leafy glade occurred on New Year's Day 1577, when the Gaelic chieftains of seven noble septs (clans) were lured here by the English, on the pretence of making peace, and all but two were slaughtered. Yet today it is a truly enchanting place, and you cannot help but fall beneath the peaceful aura that pervades the atmosphere of its sylvan depths.

Deep beneath the Rath of Mullaghmast sleeps Garrett Og Fitzgerald – 'The Wizard Earl' of Kildare – who lived at nearby Kilkea Castle and whose reputation as a practitioner of the black arts stemmed from his interest in astrology, which in the 16th century was considered little more than demonic dabbling. Despite the fact that he died and was buried in London, legend has rooted him here, where he is said to sit in a long cavern at the head of an immense banqueting table. With him sits a host of knights, clad in burnished armour, their heads resting on the table as they sleep. Behind each knight stands a milk-white steed, saddled and bridled, waiting for the day when danger casts its threatening shadow across their land.

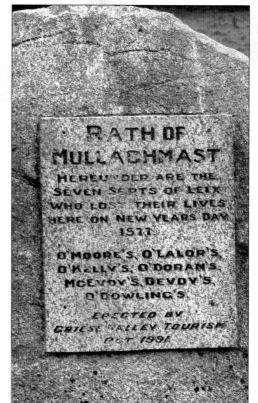

ABOVE: A memorial to an dreadful massacre that took place on New Year's Day, 1577 mars the enchanting ambience of the Rath of Mullaghmast.

Then they will ride forth to drive Ireland's enemies far from her shores. In the meantime they awake every seven years and the earl leads his mystic band of loyal warriors in procession around the Rath of Mullaghmast and thence over the fields to Kilkea Castle where, having circled his old home, they ride back to their cave and sleep again.

Those who might be tempted to question the veracity of the tale should heed the fate of the 19th-century farmer, who one night – a little the worse for drink, it must be said – was wending his way home via the Rath of Mullaghmast. He noticed that a gaping chasm, bathed in brilliant blue light, yawned open on its slopes and, venturing inside, was immediately sobered by the majestic sight of the sleeping earl and his knights. Leaning against a wall to catch his breath, he accidently knocked against a bridle, which fell to the floor with a clatter that echoed through the cave. Suddenly the earl raised his head and asked, 'Is it time yet?' Almost speechless with terror, the farmer managed to get out, 'No, your honour, not yet, but soon,' whereupon the earl placed his head back on the table, and went back to sleep.

There is no doubt that the Rath of Mullaghmast has a truly magical quality, and you really can feel close to that 'Otherworld' as you stand beneath its canopy of interlocking trees. It is easy to mistake the breeze rustling through the grass, or the glint of the sun on the early morning dew, for the movement of the fairies who, it is said, guard the Rath between the seven-year appearances of the earl and his men.

THE HILL OF TARA
The Seat of Kings
TARA, COUNTY MEATH

The hill of Tara is nothing special to look at. No crumbling ruin crowns its summit and the surrounding countryside is anything but dramatic. Yet it is a magical place, and to wander across its gentle slopes is to walk in the footsteps of gods and kings, saints and heroes.

Although legend accepts the Fir Bolg people as the first invaders to make Tara a royal seat, it was the mystical Tuatha De Danann who deemed it a sacred and godly place. They

brought with them four divine gifts, one of which, the *Lia Fail*, or Stone of Destiny, is said to be the weather-beaten monument that today stands atop the grassy mound known as the King's Seat. It was once Ireland's coronation stone, over which monarchs were crowned, which was said to emit a roar of recognition when touched by the rightful king of Tara.

It has stood here since the times when magnificent wooden palaces dominated the brow of the hill. Its memories are Ireland's memories, of ancient glories and long-ago kingships. It remembers the *feis*, those great national assemblies that took place every three years and at which laws were passed, tribal differences settled and the defence of the realm decided. It once warmed to the glow of firelight as storytellers gathered their audiences around them and, using nothing but the magic of language, spirited them away into the realm of the gods, and held them spell-bound with breathless tales of ancient conflicts and heroic conquests.

There were tales such as those of the mighty warrior, Lugh of the Long Hand, who came here to lead the Tuatha De Danann into battle against their enemies, the evil Fomorians. A warrior such as he had never been seen in Ireland before. So radiant was his countenance that when he stood upon Tara's heights, people thought the sun had risen in the west. He wore the Milky Way as a silver chain around his neck;

ABOVE: Tradition holds that only the chariot of the true King of Ireland could pass between these stones that sit on the approach to the Hill of Tara.

had a rainbow for his sling; and possessed a sword called 'the Answerer' with which he could cleave through both walls and armour. Before riding into battle at the head of a great host of warriors, he equipped himself with every magical weapon known to the world. His forces inflicted a crushing defeat upon the Fomorians and banished them from Ireland forever, after which the De Danann returned to Tara and ruled for nine generations, until the arrival from Spain of the Milesians.

Ages went by, and generations of kings were crowned over the Stone of Destiny. Then, around AD430, Loegaire became the 116th king and, during his reign, St Patrick challenged the pagan powers by lighting a pascal fire on the nearby Hill of Slane. The Druid priests warned Loegaire that if he did not extinguish the fire immediately it would burn in Ireland forever. Loegaire ignored their warnings and St Patrick came to Tara where, plucking a shamrock from the hillside, he used its three leaves and single stem to teach Loegaire about the nature of the Trinity.

All is quiet here now. The heroes have departed. The ashes of the fires by whose glowing logs the storytellers once wove

LOUGH DERRAVARAGH
The Fate of the Children of Lir
NR BALLINALACK, COUNTY WESTMEATH

One of Ireland's most poignant myths centres upon the reed-fringed shore of this remote lough. The saga began with the death in childbirth of Aobh, a stepdaughter of Bodb, king of the Tuatha De Danann, and second wife to the deity Lir. The grief-stricken Lir was left with four children – a daughter, Fionnuala, and her three brothers, Aodh, Fiachra and Conn. In an attempt to console the unfortunate widower, King Bodb offered his other stepdaughter, Aoife, as a second wife.

Aoife, however, resented the affection that Lir showered upon his children and determined to rid herself of the troublesome siblings. Realizing that she must first remove them from their father's protection, she obtained Lir's consent to take them on a visit to their grandfather. Fionnuala, however, was warned in a dream of her stepmother's evil intentions and refused to go. Lir calmed his daughter's fears, persuading her that no harm would befall them. Reassured, the children boarded Aoife's chariot to begin their ill-fated journey.

When they arrived at the shores of Lough Derravaragh, Aoife ordered her servants to kill the children. The horrified attendants refused. Unperturbed, the wicked stepmother bade her charges refresh themselves in the lough, whereupon she raised a druidic wand and cast a terrible spell upon them. A sudden flash exploded across the glassy waters, as fearsome thunder shook the earth to its core. A swirling mist descended upon the terrified children and, when the fog had cleared, they had been changed into four beautiful swans. Aoife told them that they would spend 300 years upon the lough, then a further 300 years on the Straits of Moyle (between Ireland and Scotland), followed by a final 300 years on the Atlantic Ocean. Only when they heard a Christian bell would they be transformed once more to their human shapes. She did grant them one concession: they would keep their human voices, which would be the sweetest in all of Ireland. So saying, she reined her horses and sped off to the palace of her stepfather,

ABOVE: The Mound of Hostages is just one of the many sacred relics and mythological sites that litter the tranquil summit of the Hill of Tara.

their magic have long since been raked into the hillside. The fairy folk have retreated ever further into their secret domain, driven from our consciousness by modern technology and universal conformity. It is still possible to stand upon Tara's heights and, with the breeze upon your face, imbue yourself with the spirit of the place. 'If you go there,' wrote the poet Francis Ledwidge from the mud-spattered trenches of Flanders, 'look all around you and remember me to every hill and wood and ruin, for my heart is there. Say I will come back again surely, and maybe you will hear pipes in the grass or a fairy horn – I have heard them often from Tara.'

where she informed him that she had arrived alone because Lir believed his children would be in danger if he allowed them to accompany her. However, the king was suspicious and sent messengers to Lir enquiring after the children's well-being.

The arrival of Bodb's envoys alarmed Lir and he set out in his chariot to retrace his children's journey. Passing the shores of Lough Derravaragh, he noticed four swans swimming towards him and marvelled at the sweetness of their song. Fionnuala spoke out, telling him who they were and what had happened. That night, the stricken father and his attendants camped on the shores of the lough, and his children sang to him in tones so sweet that they eased his sorrow and lulled him into a tranquil sleep.

For the next 300 years the children remained on the placid waters of Lough Derravaragh and the people of Ireland helped ease their burden by coming to visit them. Finally 900 years had passed and the swans flew ashore to return to their father's palace, but they found it a desolate ruin. Heartbroken they returned to the Western Sea and settled on the island of Inis Glora.

Meanwhile, St Patrick came to Ireland and in his wake came holy men, one of whom, St Kennock, settled on the island where the swan-children dwelt. One morning they were woken by the sound of his oratory bell and, following its chime, landed before the holy hermit, who greeted them warmly. As he did so their feathers fell away and they became human once more. They were no longer children; their bodies were stooped and wizened, their hair was white and their skin wrinkled. It was obvious that they were slowly dying. St Kennock christened them and, no sooner had he done so, they died. As the saint blessed them, four radiant children with silvery wings and tranquil expressions rose from their haggard bodies and swooped skywards to seek their place in heaven.

ABOVE: Lough Derravaragh, where the children of Lir were turned into swans by their wicked stepmother Aoife.

BELOW: The four children of Lir were condemned to spend 900 years as swans. Their only consolation was that they would retain their human voices, which would be the most beautiful in the whole of Ireland.

ROCKFLEET CASTLE
Granuaile – the Pirate Queen
NR WESTPORT, COUNTY MAYO

Gráinne O'Malley was born around 1530, the only daughter of clan chieftain Dubhdara ('Black Oak') O'Malley and his wife Margaret. They were hereditary rulers of a territory that stretched from the west coast of Ireland to the Isle of Aran and made their living by the sea. According to legend Gráinne had, as a child, begged to sail with her father, but was discouraged from doing so because a female aboard ship was considered 'Devil's ballast' – a bad omen whose presence could only induce storms and cause shipwreck. Unperturbed, she is said to have cut off all her hair and dressed in boy's clothing. This earned her the nickname 'Gráinne Mhaol' ('bald Grace'), which was later shortened to Granuaile, the sobriquet by which Irish legend and song best remember her. Thereafter she often accompanied her father on his voyages, learning his cunning, studying his ways and, ultimately, inheriting his leadership qualities.

Those qualities began to manifest themselves when, at the age of 15, Gráinne married her first husband, the ferociously quarrelsome Donal-an-Coghaidh (of the Battles) O'Flaherty. She bore him two sons, Owen and Murrough, plus a daughter, Margaret. Donal's temperament, however, was more suited to personal vendettas than to ensuring the well-being of his clan, and consequently his people were soon enduring genuine hardship. Gráinne stepped in and, by sheer force of personality, effectively made herself their chief, winning their loyalty and superseding her husband's authority. Soon afterwards, Donal was killed by his enemies and Gráinne returned to her father's territory, taking up residence at the O'Malley stronghold on Clare Island.

The only portion of Clew Bay not in O'Malley hands was the section overlooked by Rockfleet Castle. So, in 1567, Gráinne proposed marriage to the owner, Richard Bourke, suggesting that if either of them wished to withdraw from the union after one year, they would be free to do so. Tradition maintains that, at the end of one year, she locked him out of his castle and, from the ramparts, shouted, 'Richard Bourke I divorce thee.' Thereafter, the castle would be indelibly linked with her legend, and she would live there almost continuously until her death in 1603. Their divorce, however, seems to have been short-lived, since they were still married at the time of his death 16 years later.

The arrival in Ireland in 1584 of Sir Richard Bingham, newly appointed governor of Connaught, set in motion a chain of events that would culminate in Gráinne's most daring and ambitious escapade. Desperate to suppress her, Bingham engineered the murder of her eldest son and then arrested her surviving sons on charges of treason.

Gráinne boarded her ship and sailed to London where she marched into Greenwich Palace and sought an audience with Elizabeth I. In late July 1593, these two remarkable and elderly women came face to face. Elizabeth is said to have listened with a combination of admiration and sympathy, although we know nothing of what was actually discussed. Where history remains silent, legend possesses no such restraint, and the Irish talent for storytelling has subsequently blessed us with an intriguing narrative of what occurred. Gráinne is said to have sneezed and was given a richly embroidered lace handkerchief by a member of the court. Having used it she promptly cast it onto the blazing fire. When the queen reprimanded her, Gráinne retorted that the Irish would never put a soiled garment in their pocket and therefore, evidently, possessed higher standards of cleanliness than the English.

When the queen offered to make Gráinne an English countess her guest sneered dismissively. 'I don't want your titles, aren't we both equals? If there be any good in the thing I may as well make you one as you me.' And when the bemused Elizabeth defended herself against her visitor's accusation of idleness, claiming, 'I have the care of this great country on my shoulders,' she received short shrift. 'There's many a poor creature in Mayo, who has only the care of a barley field, has more industry about them than you seem to have, Queen of the English.' That Gráinne survived the audience is evidence enough that these colourful exchanges are later embellishments. The upshot of their meeting was that the queen sent word to Bingham instructing him to release his prisoners.

Gráinne's last years were relatively tame. She died at Rockfleet Castle in 1603, and was buried in the Cistercian abbey on Clare Island.

ANTRIM CASTLE GARDENS
Lady Marion's Wolfhound
COUNTY ANTRIM

In the picturesque gardens of Antrim Castle, little of which now survives, stands a stone wolfhound behind whose petrified form lies a poignant and colourful legend. In the early 1600s, Sir Hugh Clotworthy brought his beautiful young bride, Marion of the Tresses, to live at the fort he had constructed in Antrim. Despite the idyllic surroundings, it proved a lonely existence for the young woman. Her husband was frequently absent for long periods on military business and she found herself pining for the bygone days of her girlhood, spent with a loving family and close friends at Carrickfergus Castle.

OPPOSITE: Rockfleet Castle, once the home of Ireland's legendary pirate queen Granuaile, was an ideal base for her to make money from charging protection for the safe passage of shipping.

Accepting her lot, she sought solitary consolation by wandering through the sylvan grounds of her new home. One day, as she made her way through a particularly thickly wooded copse, she was stopped in her tracks by a low, menacing growl. Suddenly, a savage wolf sprang from the bush and knocked her to the ground. Terror-stricken, Marion fainted.

She awoke to an incredible sight. The savaged body of the wolf lay beside her and a large Irish wolfhound, itself badly injured, was standing guard over her. Realizing that the dog had saved her life, she took him back to the fort. Her servants tended his wounds and Marion nursed him back to health. Having made a full recovery, the hound disappeared and, despite a thorough search of the area, no trace of him could be found.

The years went by, and Sir Hugh Clotworthy gradually turned their abode into a grand castle. Then, one storm-tossed night, as the wind howled through the nooks and crannies of the fortress and the rain pelted its walls, a loud baying was heard over the tempest, awaking those asleep within the castle walls. As the lightning streaked across the heavens, it illuminated the unmistakable form of the faithful wolfhound, and Marion let out a cry of delighted recognition. At that moment the garrison spotted an enemy force moving towards the castle, evidently hoping to take it by surprise. A fierce battle ensued, which saw the defenders repel their attackers; but in the closing moments of the fracas, a loud agonized yelp was heard over the gunfire.

With the castle safe and the assailants fled, Marion rushed to the spot from which the wolfhound had sounded his warning only to find an untidy heap of flattened musket balls and a trail of congealed blood disappearing into the woods. She followed it to make strange and curious discovery: for on the ground lay the Irish bloodhound, but it had somehow been turned to stone.

Sir Hugh Clotworthy had the petrified beast carried back to Antrim Castle and, recognizing the effigy's potential to repel superstitious enemies, mounted it atop one of the castle's towers, from where it gazed out across the surrounding countryside until the building's destruction in 1922. Thereafter it rested at sundry sites around the grounds before settling at its current location on one of the castle's beautiful lawns.

THE GIANT'S CAUSEWAY
Finn McCool
NR BUSHMILLS, COUNTRY ANTRIM

The Giant's Causeway is a weird mass of some 40,000, mostly hexagonal, basalt columns, which form a series of stepping-stones stretching from the base of the cliffs and disappearing into the sea off the north Antrim coast. They result from a series of

violent underground volcanic explosions that took place some 60 million years ago. There is a strange, almost otherworldly feel about the place or, as William Makepeace Thackeray put it, 'when the world was moulded and fashioned out of formless chaos, this must have been the bit over, a remnant of chaos.'

Of course the Irish love of storytelling has long blessed the Causeway with supernatural rather than natural origins, and tradition has attributed its creation to the giant Finn McCool, also known as Finn Mac Cumaill. Epic myths abound detailing the exploits of this legendary figure and his select band of warrior followers, known as the Fianna or Fenians. In the stories concerning his building of the Giant's Causeway, he is described as dwelling on the draughty Antrim headland, where he 'lived most happy and content, obeyed no law and paid no rent.' One story has him falling in love with a giantess on Staffa, an island in the Hebrides, and building this wide and spacious highway in order that she might join him in Ulster.

Another account holds that, across the sea in Scotland, there lived a rival giant named Benandonner. He and Finn would often stand on their respective shorelines hurling insults at each other. Then one day Benandonner challenged his rival to a show of strength, and the ever-obliging Finn

ABOVE: The Giant's Causeway, one of Ireland's most famous natural sites, that legend attributes to the legendary giant Finn Mac Cumaill.

OPPOSITE: A large Irish wolfhound protected Marion Clotworthy from a savage wolf, and is commemorated by a stone statue in Antrim Castle Gardens.

built a rocky causeway from County Antrim to the island of Staffa to aid his adversary in crossing the sea. The work, however, proved so strenuous that, having completed it, Finn fell asleep. The next morning Oonagh, Finn's wife, was woken by the sound of heavy footsteps and spied the Scottish giant hurrying over the Causeway towards them. Unable to wake her husband, she covered his sleeping form with her shawl and bonnet. 'Where's that coward hiding?' thundered Benandonner, looking down upon the sleeping Finn. 'He's away,' replied Oonagh, 'and I'll thank you to keep your voice down, so as you don't waken the baby.' A look of horror dawned upon Benadonner's face. 'If his baby's this big,' he whispered, 'I'm not waiting to meet Finn, for he must be immense.' With that he ran back across the Causeway, destroying it as he went, so that all that now remains is this section just off the Antrim headland.

THE NORSEMEN COMETH

But in green ruins, in the desolate walls
Of antique palaces, where Man hath been,
Though the dun fox or wild hyena calls,
And owls, that flit continually between,
Shriek to the echo, and the low winds moan –
There the true Silence is, self-conscious and alone.

FROM *SILENCE*
BY THOMAS HOOD (1798–1845)

LANCASHIRE, NORTH YORKSHIRE, CUMBRIA, TYNE & WEAR, & NORTHUMBERLAND

From the urban spread of industrial Lancashire, through to the peaceful serenity of the Lake District, across the tranquil enchantment of Yorkshire to the wild and untamed splendour of the Northumberland coast, the north of England revels in a stunning panorama of scenic variety and legendary landscapes. On the northeast coast in the 7th century, a golden age held sway as people such as St Aidan and St Cuthbert brought Christianity to the ancient Kingdom of Northumberland. Then, in the 8th century, Viking raiders swept in from the sea, bringing with them tales of dragons, ogres, trolls and demon hounds. They introduced these horrors to the mysterious places that local legend had already imbued with evil and sinister reputations. Many of the Vikings settled, and their descendants became the ferocious cattle stealers, or reivers, who terrorized the lands around the border with Scotland throughout the Middle Ages and on into the 18th century. The consequence of this rich mixture of so many different cultures is today evident in the wonderful variety of lore and legend that the North has to offer.

KEY

1. Pendle Hill
2. All Saints' Church
3. Whitby Abbey
4. Clifford's Tower
5. Millennium Gallery
6. Hylton Castle
7. Lambton Castle
8. Holy Island

ABOVE: Lancaster Castle, which the so-called Pendle Witches confessed to conspiring to blow up by magic, and where they were later imprisoned before being executed.

RIGHT: The Lancashire witches, with their animal familiars at their feet, gather around a bubbling cauldron to cast their spells and curses

PREVIOUS PAGES: Lindisfarne Castle, which stands on one of England's most spiritually charged places, Holy Island, was once the cradle of northern Christianity.

PENDLE HILL
The Pendle Witches
NR CLITHEROE, LANCASHIRE

In the early years of the 17th century there lived on the brooding slopes of Pendle Hill two feuding families headed by two matriarchs known locally as 'Mother Demdike' and 'Old Chattox'. Both families had a sinister reputation as witches, and were much feared by those living roundabouts. In March 1612, Demdike's granddaughter, Alizon Device, met a tinker named John Law whom she asked for some pins. When he refused to undo his pack, Alizon cursed him. Unfortunately, no sooner had the words left her mouth, than the man suffered a stroke. Alizon was arrested and charged with witchcraft. Amazingly, she not only admitted her

own guilt, but also implicated several members of both her own and Chattox's families. Soon both Demdike and Chattox found themselves charged with witchcraft, whilst Alizon's mother, Bessie, was stripped and discovered to possess a third nipple, a sure sign that she was suckling a demonic familiar. When questioned by the local magistrate, Roger Nowell, Demdike and Chattox both confessed to and accused each other of an extraordinary variety of imaginative crimes. These included the desecration of graves, communing with Satan, plotting to blow up Lancaster Castle by magic and at least 16 murders. They also revealed the existence of seven further witches in the neighbourhood, including Alice Nutter, a gentlewoman from nearby Roughlee Hall. Quite why they were so willing to admit to such preposterous charges has never been ascertained. Perhaps they saw their interrogations as a convenient opportunity to settle the feud that had raged between their families for more than ten years.

Demdike died in prison, but the others, having been found guilty of witchcraft, were sentenced to death. The judge's comment that he had been moved by 'the ruine of so many poore creatures at one time' was of little solace to the so-called 'Pendle Witches', who were executed before a large crowd on Thursday 20th August, 1612.

ALL SAINTS' CHURCH
The Rudston Monolith
RUDSTON, NORTH YORKSHIRE

Standing an impressive 7.6 metres (25 feet) high, and dwarfing the adjacent church, the Rudston Monolith is the tallest standing stone in Britain. Its rain-washed bulk is thought to have stood here since 1600BC, and its original purpose is not known. Some say it was a fertility symbol and its phallic nature might give credence to such a theory. Indeed, a local belief says that if a man touches the stone with his wedding ring on three successive nights when the moon is waxing, he will become a more effective lover.

One of the paradoxes of the stone is why such a blatantly pagan symbol was allowed to remain when the church was built. Perhaps the native religion centred upon the stone had such a powerful grip on the community that the church had little choice but to co-exist with it. Or maybe the stone, which tradition maintains extends as far beneath the ground as it does above, was too immense for the church founders to remove. The church then had to either Christianize or demonize the monument, and several legends attest to the attempts of bygone incumbents to do just that. One story maintains that the stone simply fell straight from the sky one day 'killing certain desecrators of the churchyard.' Another says that the stone arrived in the churchyard when the Devil, annoyed at the building of the church on a hill that he held sacred, hurled a stone javelin at the building. Thanks, however,

to divine intervention, the missile was deflected and became embedded in the ground alongside the church. It stands there to this very day.

WHITBY ABBEY
St Hilda and the Serpents
WHITBY, NORTH YORKSHIRE

Never is the Gothic splendour of Whitby Abbey so impressive, its impact so dramatic, as on a tempest-tossed night when a murderous gale howls in from the grey North Sea and

ABOVE: The massive Rudston Monolith stands alongside All Saints Church. It is a mystery as to why the church authorities allowed such an obviously pagan symbol to survive and dwarf their church.

drives the raging waves in frenzied assault against the steadfast cliffs. During such storms, the tattered remnants of the once-mighty abbey seem to shudder with the onslaught, and it is easy to see how this formidable clifftop ruin provided the backdrop for the opening of Bram Stoker's *Dracula*.

By choosing Whitby as the place where Dracula landed in England, Stoker bestowed upon this timeless fishing port a sinister immortality on which it has capitalized ever since. Standing amongst the sombre grey-brown tombstones in the clifftop churchyard of St Mary's, and gazing down upon the red-tiled roofs, cobblestone streets and sea-washed harbour walls of the town beneath, one is immediately struck by how

little the vista has changed since Bram Stoker found inspiration here. Long before Count Dracula came padding ashore in the guise of a huge black dog, the stark ruins of Whitby Abbey had mellowed into a ripe dotage, and legends aplenty had begun to swirl around its hallowed walls.

Oswy, King of Northumbria, founded the monastery of Streoneshalh, from which Whitby Abbey evolved, in AD657,

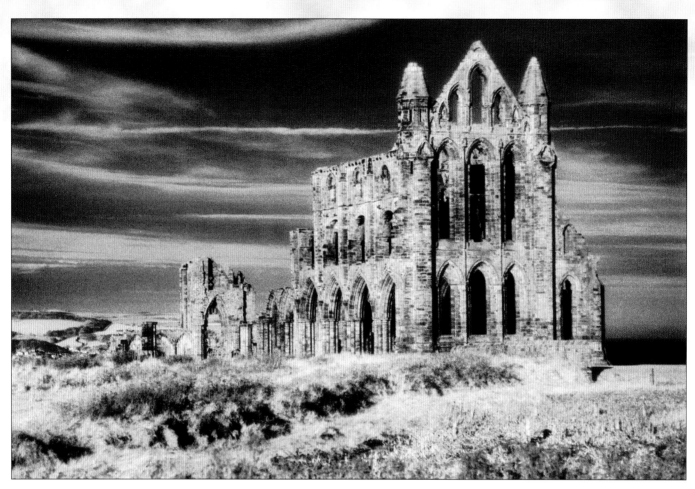

ABOVE: Whitby Abbey, amongst whose ragged vestiges Count Dracula first set foot on English soil in the guise of a hideous black dog.

OPPOSITE: The red stains that once appeared on the walls of Clifford's Tower were associated with a shameful and barbaric act that took place in March 1190.

and St Hilda, a member of the royal house, was appointed as its first abbess. When she arrived at the spot where the abbey was to be built, she found the whole clifftop infested with poisonous snakes. She drove these to the cliff edge and, as they tumbled over, sliced off their heads with her whip, causing them to curl into tiny balls. The fossil ammonites – small and coiled, serpent-like creatures dating from the Jurassic period – that are found on the beach beneath the abbey (and that have been incorporated into the Whitby coat of arms) are reputed to be the petrified remnants of these snakes.

In AD664, the famous Synod of Whitby was held at the monastery, and representatives of the Celtic and Roman Churches came here to resolve such important matters as fixing a date for Easter. In AD867, the Danes sacked the monastery and it lay desolate for the next 200 years until its resurrection as a Benedictine foundation in 1074. By the end of the 12th century, the magnificent abbey, the ruins of which crown the clifftop today, had been built.

Thereafter its history was uneventful until its dissolution in 1540, when the lead was stripped from its roofs and the bells removed, taken to the harbour and loaded onto a ship bound for London. The vessel suddenly sank and the bells have never

been recovered. Legend, however, deems it a good omen for lovers to hear their ghostly peal, sounding from beneath the waves, on the night before Halloween.

CLIFFORD'S TOWER
The Bloody Walls
YORK, NORTH YORKSHIRE

In 1068 William the Conqueror headed for York, intent on crushing Saxon resistance. On the summit of a large mound in the city centre he erected a simple wooden tower, which Henry II later expanded. A century or so later, in March 1190, an anti-Jewish riot erupted in the streets of York, and many of the city's Jews took refuge behind the seemingly impregnable walls of the castle. However, the rioters, led by a man named Richard Malebisse, set fire to the tower, and the terror-stricken Jews, faced with either burning to death or taking their chances against the howling mob outside, chose to commit mass suicide.

The castle was rebuilt in timber and then, during the reign of King John, work was begun on a stone fortress, which was

MILLENNIUM GALLERY
The Reivers' Curse
CARLISLE, CUMBRIA

ABOVE: Carlisle's cursing stone is inscribed with the words of a curse that the Bishop of Glasgow once aimed at the notorious border reivers.

From the 14th to the late 17th centuries, the ever-shifting border between England and Scotland was a wild and lawless frontier whose residents lived in constant fear of the savage Border reivers. With the authorities powerless against them, and with more and more families being left bereaved, it fell to the Church, in the robust shape of Gavin Dunbar, Archbishop of Glasgow, to adopt a more temporal means of dealing with the threat. In 1525, Dunbar excommunicated all Border reivers and devised one of the most comprehensive curses of all time. Each Sunday the priests in every pulpit of Cumbria, Northumberland, the Borders, Dumfries and Galloway were instructed to recite the archbishop's tirade to their congregations. A modernized extract reads:

> I curse their head and all the hairs of their head;
> I curse their face, their mouth, their tongue, their teeth
> Their breast, their heart, their stomach, their back, their hands, their feet
> And every part of their bodies.
> I curse their wives, their babies, and their servants;
> I condemn them perpetually to the deep pit of hell.

The curse would probably have remained a distant folk memory had Carlisle City Council not had it engraved onto a giant 'cursing stone' and made it the centrepiece of their underground millennium gallery. This provoked fierce criticism from Cumbria's Christian community, some of whom came to see it as the cause of the foot and mouth epidemic that devastated the district in 2001. 'Clearly the council holds matters spiritual in such trivial regard,' wrote a vicar in his parish magazine, 'that it can cheerfully commission the equivalent of a loaded gun and regard it as a tourist attraction.' Meanwhile, a council spokesperson defended their actions. 'We do not regard the stone as evil,' she said. 'We regard it as a work of public art.'

HYLTON CASTLE
The Cauld Lad
NR CASTLETOWN, TYNE AND WEAR

The hollow shell of its gatehouse is all that remains of Hylton Castle. Yet it possesses a timelessness that no amount of urban encroachment can dispel. Although Baron William Hylton built the castle in the early 15th century, the events behind its legend occurred some 300 years later when it

completed by Henry III. In 1322, the royal forces defeated a Lancastrian army at Boroughbridge and one of the rebel leaders, Roger de Clifford, was hung in chains from the tower. Soon afterwards the building acquired the name by which it is still known: Clifford's Tower.

Not long after the castle's transformation into the impressive stone edifice that overlooks the city today, unsightly red stains began to appear on its walls. The people of York quickly connected these to the Jewish suicides of 130 years before and were soon whispering in guilty tones that the blood of the dead Jews had caused the blemishes. Although in recent years it has been shown that the discoloration is caused by the presence of minute quantities of iron oxide, or rust, in the stone, the fact remains that no other stone from the Tadcaster quarry that supplied it contains any trace of such minerals!

became the haunt of that most useful of household spirits, a brownie.

In his 1597 *Daemonologie,* James VI and I defined a brownie as a Devil that, having taken the appearance of a naked and hairy man, would haunt 'divers houses, without doing any evill, but doing as it were necessarie turnes up and down the house.' Quite naturally, most people were delighted to find their abode haunted by a spirit that would perform all manner of domestic chores, and would take care not to drive their nocturnal visitor away. Reginald Scott, in his *Discoverie of Witchcraft* (1584), warned that 'if the maid or good wife of the house, having compassion of his nakedness, laid any clothes for him', then the brownie would never return.

Hylton Castle's brownie was known as the 'Cauld Lad', and there is a tradition that maintains he was the ghost of a stable boy, murdered by a tyrannical 18th-century owner of the castle. Whatever his origin, the servants, who slept in the great tower, would hear him working away in the kitchens each night and, next morning, would find the day's food prepared and yesterday's dirty utensils washed and put away. Should the servants leave no chores for the Cauld Lad, however, he would show his displeasure by smashing crockery, mixing the salt and sugar together, and filling the flour bin with ashes.

Perhaps it was this latter behaviour that decided the servants to get rid of him and, having fashioned a cloak and hood from the finest Lincoln green cloth, they laid it out in the kitchen and concealed themselves to watch what would happen. At midnight, the Cauld Lad appeared and was obviously overjoyed by the garment. The servants watched him put it on and then dance around the kitchen, singing:

> *Here's a cloak, and here's a hood,*
> *The Cauld Lad of Hylton will do no more good.*

Thereafter the brownie was never seen again.

LAMBTON CASTLE
The Lambton Worm
NR PENSHAW, TYNE AND WEAR

At the time of the Crusades, John Henshaw was heir to the lordship of Lambton. He was a wild and unruly lad, who preferred to spend Sunday mornings fishing on the leafy banks of the River Wear rather than attending church with the rest of his family. One day he caught the most hideous creature he

ABOVE: Hylton Castle once had a useful brownie that would do all the household chores during the night.

had ever seen. It was a small, wormlike thing with the head of a salamander and razor-sharp teeth. With a grimace of disgust, he plopped his catch into his basket and, as he reached the drive to Lambton Castle, tipped the mysterious creature into an ancient well by the gates.

Years later, having forsaken his wild ways, John Henshaw set off to fight in the Crusades. Meanwhile, in the dark and slimy depths of its watery lair, the creature grew, and took to setting out at night to sate its ferocious appetite. Shepherds came across half-eaten sheep littering the fields each morning, and the cows of the district yielded less and less milk. Mystified by the bizarre occurrences, the lord of the castle sent two servants to keep watch one night and, next morning, the terrified men told how they had seen a frightful serpent come slithering from the well at dead of night. Soon the Lambton Worm was terrorizing the neighbourhood, killing man and beast alike. Many brave men

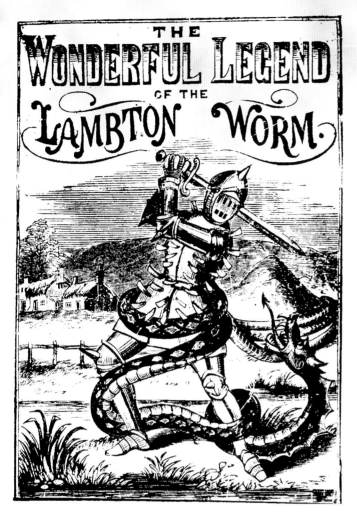

THE WONDERFUL LEGEND OF THE LAMBTON WORM

ABOVE: Sir John Lambton slays the dreaded serpent that his folly had leased upon the neighbourhood.

but she waved him back and, fixing him with a cold stare, warned him: 'Fail to do so and you will bring a curse upon your family whereby nine generations of Lambtons will not die peacefully in their beds.' When he told his father what had transpired the two men hatched a plan whereby, if he succeeded in killing the worm, John would blow loudly on his horn as a signal to his father to release the castle dogs, one of whom he would kill.

The following day, attired as the witch had instructed, John settled himself on the riverbank and awaited the arrival of his adversary. Presently its formidable outline slithered into view and, as it entered the water, the fearless knight attacked. Furiously the creature lashed its tail, sending a wall of water towards him. Steeling himself against the tide, John lunged forward, raised his sword and brought it down hard. As pieces of the worm were hacked off, they were carried away by the current. In its frenzy, the monster lunged at John and, coiling itself around him, attempted to crush him to death, but the razors cut deep into its flesh until, finally, it closed its eyes and its carcass was swept away on the tide.

Exhausted, the victorious knight crawled onto the bank and blew a mighty blast upon his horn. His father was so excited when he heard it that he forgot to release the hounds and instead raced to congratulate his son. Unable to kill his father John laid down his sword, and the two men realized that their family would be cursed forevermore.

> **'YOU WILL BRING A CURSE UPON YOUR FAMILY WHEREBY NINE GENERATIONS OF LAMBTONS WILL NOT DIE PEACEFULLY IN THEIR BEDS.'**
>
> THE WITCH WARNS JOHN HENSHAW, THE WORM SLAYER

neighbourhood, killing man and beast alike. Many brave men tried to destroy it, but whenever their swords hacked it in two the pieces simply crawled back together and joined up again.

When John Henshaw returned he was stricken with guilt and consulted a local witch as to how he might rid the district of the scourge his youthful folly had unleashed. 'You must stud your armour with razor-sharp spears and knives,' she told him, 'and you must ensure that you only fight the creature in the river, for then and only then shall you kill it.' John thanked her and asked what he owed her for the information. 'I ask nothing,' she replied. 'But you must promise that you will kill the first creature to greet you after the worm is dead.' Promising her that he would do so, he got up to leave;

HOLY ISLAND
St Cuthbert
NORTHUMBERLAND

The 7th century was the golden age for Northumbria, the Anglo-Saxon kingdom that stretched from the Humber to the Forth and whose capital was Bamburgh. There the castle of the Northumbrian Kings, on its massive whinstone crag, gazed across the sea to Lindisfarne, the Holy Island from which Christianity was spread throughout the territory.

In AD635 King Oswald summoned Aidan to Bamburgh from the island of Iona, and charged him with the task of converting his subjects to Christianity. Aidan based himself on the island of Lindisfarne from where he went forth to preach his message.

In AD642, Oswald was slain in battle by Penda of Mercia, champion of the pagan gods who, determined to force the old religion back upon the people of Northumbria, besieged Bamburgh. From Lindisfarne Aidan watched as Penda stacked piles of wood against the castle walls, intending to burn it down. 'See, Lord,' he prayed, 'what ill Penda worketh.' Suddenly the wind changed direction, blowing clouds of smoke and fire into the faces of the would-be attackers, and the castle was saved.

It is, however, with St Cuthbert, who came to the island in AD665, that Lindisfarne is most closely identified. He worked on the island for 12 years and was much loved and respected by the monks. Then, wishing to further dedicate himself to a life of prayer, he withdrew alone to the Farne Islands and, on the one that now bears his name, lived as a hermit for nine years, during which time his sanctity became famous throughout Europe. He returned in AD685 to assume the Bishopric of Lindisfarne, but two years later, worn out by a life of self-mortification, he died. He was buried in the priory church, where his body became one of the monks' most treasured possessions. The monastery became famed as one of the greatest centres of art and learning in Europe, and the monks lived contented in secure piety, dedicating themselves to creating items of stunning craftsmanship, such as the exquisitely beautiful Lindisfarne Gospels.

This golden age of Christian culture ended abruptly with the coming of the Vikings. In AD793, according to the *Anglo-Saxon*

ABOVE: Holy Island's monastic ruins belie the fact that this place was once renowned as one of the greatest centres of art and learning in Europe.

BELOW: Much of the stone from the great abbey on Holy Island was used to build Lindisfarne Castle, which enjoys a dramatic setting.

Chronicle, 'terrible portents appeared over Northumbria... and a little while after that the harrying of the heathen miserably destroyed God's church in Lindisfarne.'

When, in AD875, the Danes ravaged the island for a second time, the monks fled, carrying with them St Cuthbert's body. For over a century the holy relics were moved from place to place, once even returning to Lindisfarne for a year, until they found a permanent resting place in Durham Cathedral.

Nothing now remains of the Saxon church and monastery on Lindisfarne, save mouldering fragments of stone and time-worn grave slabs. The Benedictine priory, the massive sandstone pillars and graceful arches of which totter in ruin close to the shoreline, was founded in the 12th century. The island itself can only be reached at low tide, via a 4.8 kilometre (3-mile) causeway that twists across a forlorn wilderness of shimmering mudflats and delivers you to what is, without doubt, a sacred and magical place.

MONSTERS, PROPHETS and HIGHLAND LEGENDS

O Caledonia! stern and wild,
Meet nurse for a poetic child!
Land of brown heath and shaggy wood,
Land of the mountain and the flood,
Land of my sires! what mortal hand
Can e'er untie the filial band
That knits me to thy rugged strand!

FROM *THE PATRIOT*

BY SIR WALTER SCOTT (1771–1832)

SCOTLAND

Scotland's beauty is legendary. Its magnificent mountains, serene lochs, lonely glens, tumbling rivers, gentle pastures and vast wildernesses can unfetter the mind and stir the soul of even the most jaded. It is a country of contrasts with a complex and varied past. For centuries Scotland was a divided nation and its history is spattered with the blood of countless conflicts, many fought between Highlanders and Lowlanders. Yet it possesses an ethereal landscape that is home to an array of heroes, giants, earth goddesses, fearsome monsters and the wee folk, or fairies. It is this combination of brutal history and otherworldly enchantment that have made Scotland a land of legend. One moment you can be gazing into the serene waters of a tranquil loch, or sitting amidst brooding hills pondering a tale of ancient mystery; the next you can be crossing a field where thousands died in some bloody battle or brutal massacre.

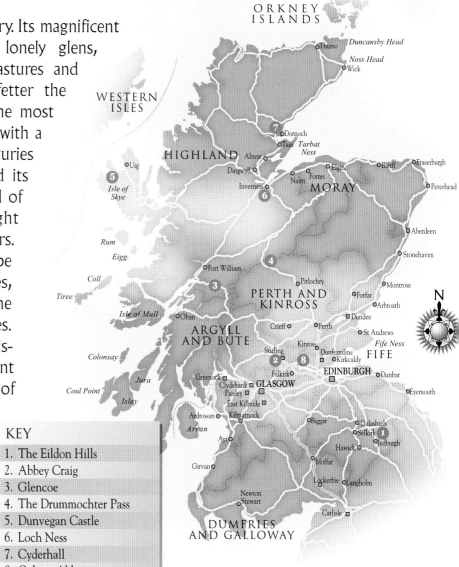

KEY

1. The Eildon Hills
2. Abbey Craig
3. Glencoe
4. The Drummochter Pass
5. Dunvegan Castle
6. Loch Ness
7. Cyderhall
8. Culross Abbey

THE EILDON HILLS
Thomas the Rhymer
NR MELROSE, BORDERS

An unremarkable stone marks the spot where one of the most beautiful Scottish romances is said to have begun. Thomas of Erceldourne (1220–97) was resting here one day when he met with the Queen of Fairyland, who bade him join her on her milk-white steed, whereupon she took him to the gates of Fairyland. Here she paused and warned Thomas that during his

time inside he must not utter a single word, no matter what marvels he beheld. With that they entered an enchanted land, bathed in dazzling light.

For seven years Thomas served the Fairy Queen, and during all that time he spoke not a word. When the day came for him to leave, his mistress plucked an apple from a tree as a reward, promising that it would bestow upon him the gift of prophecy and a tongue that could never lie. As they said goodbye she told him that one day she would send two messengers to call him back. Over the years, Thomas travelled all

over Scotland, pronouncing his prophecies. He is said to have predicted the death of Alexander III of Scotland, the Battle of Bannockburn and the accession of James VI to the throne of England. His fame spread far and wide and he became immensely wealthy. He was always restless, for he truly missed Fairyland and longed to be with his queen once more. When he was an old man, his servants came rushing to tell him that they had seen a milk-white hart and hind coming towards the house. Knowing them to be the messengers that his mistress had spoken of, Thomas happily went with them into the forest and was never seen again.

ABBEY CRAIG
The Wallace Memorial and the Battle of Stirling Bridge
NR STIRLING, STIRLING

On 10th September 1297, William Wallace stood upon the lofty heights of Abbey Craig – site of Scotland's national memorial to him – and gazed across the River Forth at the English-held stronghold of Stirling Castle. The second son of minor Scottish noble Malcolm Wallace, William had grown up against the background of war, intrigue and ruthless oppression that had seen Scotland's king, John Balliol, stripped of his sovereignty by England's Edward I.

By his mid twenties, William, standing over 2 metres (6 feet) tall, was a giant in both stature and reputation. He had avenged the killing of his father by murdering the English knight responsible, and was living as an outlaw, waging a ruthless

ABOVE: It was amid the splendour of the Eildon Hills that Thomas of Erceldourne is reputed to have met with the Queen of the Fairies and to have gone with her into Elfland.

PREVIOUS PAGES: Dunvegan Castle on the Isle of Skye is the oldest inhabited castle in Scotland.

guerrilla campaign against the English. He was also betrothed to the beautiful heiress Marion Braidfute, who lived in the town of Lanark. When the English Sheriff of Lanark, Hazelrig, had Marion's brother executed, Wallace and his comrades set out to avenge the killing and achieved this by putting 50 English soldiers to the sword.

Unable to get at Wallace, Hazelrig had Marion executed instead. It was an ill-conceived act of barbaric injustice and it brought the full wrath of William Wallace crashing into town. He and his followers murdered the sheriff and slaughtered 240 of its English residents. With Lanark still smouldering from this retribution, Wallace went on the rampage, plundering his way across Scotland, collecting fables and followers as he went. By the time he arrived upon Abbey Craig, his army had swollen to over 40,000 men.

From Stirling Castle the English commander, William de Warrenne, watched the rebels assemble. With 50,000 seasoned and heavily armed soldiers, he was confident that the ill-disciplined, lightly armed Scottish force would be easily defeated. Observing battle protocol, he sent two friars to offer a reprieve if Wallace and his comrades would surrender. 'Tell your commander that we are here not to make peace but to do battle, to defend ourselves,' was Wallace's contemptuous reply. 'Let them come on and we shall prove this in their very beards.'

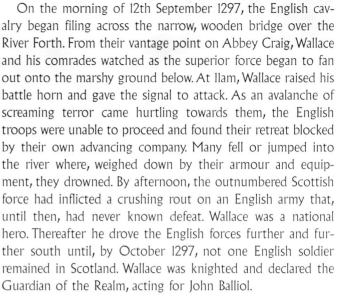

On the morning of 12th September 1297, the English cavalry began filing across the narrow, wooden bridge over the River Forth. From their vantage point on Abbey Craig, Wallace and his comrades watched as the superior force began to fan out onto the marshy ground below. At 11am, Wallace raised his battle horn and gave the signal to attack. As an avalanche of screaming terror came hurtling towards them, the English troops were unable to proceed and found their retreat blocked by their own advancing company. Many fell or jumped into the river where, weighed down by their armour and equipment, they drowned. By afternoon, the outnumbered Scottish force had inflicted a crushing rout on an English army that, until then, had never known defeat. Wallace was a national hero. Thereafter he drove the English forces further and further south until, by October 1297, not one English soldier remained in Scotland. Wallace was knighted and declared the Guardian of the Realm, acting for John Balliol.

The following year, Edward I mustered a huge fighting force and, on 12th July 1298, routed the Scots at Falkirk. The rebellion was over and, although he managed to escape from the battlefield, Wallace renounced his guardianship and faded into obscurity. In 1305, betrayed by one of his own countrymen, he was captured and taken to London. There, on 23rd August 1305, he was dragged through the streets to suffer the barbaric fate of being hanged, drawn and quartered.

GLENCOE
The Weeping Glen
GLENCOE, HIGHLAND

The Macdonalds of Glencoe were as fearsome and ruthless a tribe as any other in the bloody history of inter-clan rivalry and warfare. Their officially sanctioned massacre at the hands of the Campbells caused such a deep sense of outrage that even their bitterest enemies viewed it with undisguised revulsion. This wasn't just murder; this was 'murder under trust' and, as such, it broke a moral code to which even the most brutish clan adhered. For it was an inviolable custom of the Highlands that you should provide hospitality to anyone who sought it, be they friend or foe.

It all began in December 1691 when, in a determined effort to bring the Jacobite Highlanders to heel, the authorities in Edinburgh decreed that, before the year's end, every clan must swear an oath of allegiance to King William III. The majority made the pledge immediately, but prominent amongst those who didn't were the Macdonalds of Glencoe, whose chief, Alasdair Macdonald, made the fatal error of holding out until the last possible moment. When he finally decided to swear,

LEFT: The statue of William Wallace proudly adorns Scotland's memorial to him at Abbey Craig, where he led his forces to resounding victory at the Battle of Stirling Bridge.

an unfortunate combination of tragic error, bureaucratic obstinacy and atrocious winter conditions meant he was several days late. Sir John Dalrymple, Secretary of State for Scotland, seized the opportunity to make an example of him and his clan.

At the beginning of February 1692, Captain Robert Glenlyon was ordered to lead 120 men of the Earl of Argyle's Regiment – all Campbells, and hereditary enemies of the Macdonalds – into Glencoe. John Macdonald, the elder son of the chief, came to meet them, and demanded the reason for a military force entering a peaceful territory. Glenlyon explained that they came as friends and merely sought suitable quarters against the winter snows. Thereupon they received a warm welcome and were afforded food and lodgings. On the evening of 12th February the duplicitous Glenlyon settled down to a game of cards with his host's family. All the while he had in his pocket the clan's brutal death warrant, instructing him to 'fall upon the rebels of Glencoe, and put all to the sword under the age of seventy.'

At precisely five o'clock the next morning, a sudden explosion of rifle fire shattered the silence of the frozen glen. The old chief was shot dead as he rose from his bed, and his wife so cruelly abused that she died of her injuries the following day. As the first rays of dawn stretched across the grisly scene, the snow was red with Macdonald blood, and 38 members of the clan

> **'YOU ARE HEREBY ORDERED TO FALL UPON THE REBELS, THE MACDONALDS OF GLENCOE, AND TO PUT ALL TO THE SWORD UNDER THE AGE OF SEVENTY.'**
>
> THE GOVERNMENT ORDER TO CAPTAIN GLENLYON

ABOVE: Glencoe –the Weeping Glen – still has an uneasy feeling about it as though the very air is imbued with the notoriety of the brutal massacre of the Macdonalds.

lay butchered. The great majority, however, evaded their pursuers and hundreds of men, women and children escaped into the mountains. They were ill-equipped for their flight; many were overcome by the bitter winter temperatures, or else floundered in the deep snows where they perished miserably.

Today a chilling aura of indefinable restlessness hangs heavy over what is truly one of Britain's most poignant and haunting landscapes. Every nook, crevice and cranny seems imbued with the terror and hopeless sorrow that washed across the valley on that morning. Indeed, such is the stark and fearsome beauty of the place that it is possible to agree wholeheartedly with Charles Dickens' sentiment that 'anything so bleak and wild and mighty in its loneliness, it is impossible to conceive.'

THE DRUMMOCHTER PASS
Michael Scott
NR NEWTONMORE, HIGHLAND

Michael Scott is one of those mysterious figures about whom little is known, but whose reputation is firmly implanted in the annals of folklore. He was a widely travelled medieval philosopher and scientist, who served as the court astrologer to Emperor Frederick II and who may, or may not, be buried in Melrose Abbey.

ABOVE: It was on the Drummochter Pass that the enigmatic wizard, Michael Scott, slew the dragon and was subsequently given the gift of knowing all things about all men.

OPPOSITE: Dunvegan Castle, home to the Macleods' Fairy Flag, which will keep the clan safe in times of trouble.

As a young man he and two companions were travelling one day through the Pass of Drummochter, when a huge white serpent attacked them. His friends ran for their lives, but Michael Scott stood his ground and managed to slay the creature. Having hacked the serpent into three pieces, he called his friends back and, taking one segment each, they set off for Dalwhinnie to spend the night at an inn. Here they talked of nothing but their encounter, and the landlord offered a free night's accommodation in return for the middle segment of the serpent. Michael, who owned it, agreed and the landlord gave it to his wife to make a broth.

As the blubbery mass simmered over the fire, Michael, curious as to what serpent stew would taste like, went into the kitchen and licked the spoon being used to stir the concoction. Instantly he was blessed with the gift of knowing all things. He could speak the language of bird and beast, knew how to raise and command the Devil, and understood astrology, science and alchemy. He knew all things about all men and, with his new-found ability to see into the future, realized that the innkeeper would kill him for stealing the power of the serpent. Therefore he and his companions did a moonlight flit and Michael, now the greatest wizard in the whole of Europe, embarked upon his travels.

Years later, withered by age and knowing that death was close, he is said to have returned to these hills where his friends summoned a priest to give him the last rites. Such was his reputation as a practitioner of the black arts, however, that the minister refused. 'To hell you belong and to hell you will go' was the only blessing he would bestow. Scott asked his friends to hang his heart from the branch of a nearby fir tree. 'If a raven carries it off, you will know that the priest spoke the truth. But if a dove comes for it you will know that I spoke the truth when I said that my powers were used only for good, and that God has forgiven me my sins as a man.' So saying he died and his friends buried him. No sooner had they hung up his heart than a raven came swooping down, talons bared, to seize it. A sudden flash of light startled the bird and it flew away. A dove then appeared and, clasping the heart, lifted it from the tree and flew off. Thus was the Devil — whom tradition holds was at that moment preparing a bed of white-hot rock for Michael Scott in the Grampian mountains — denied his prize, and thus also was the judgemental priest said to have been 'somewhat put about'.

DUNVEGAN CASTLE
The Fairy Flag of the Macleods
ISLE OF SKYE, HIGHLAND

Dunvegan Castle, parts of which may date from the 9th century, is the oldest inhabited castle in Scotland and is the hereditary home of the clan Macleod, whose chiefs claim descent from the Norse Kings of Man and the Western Isles. The fortress itself is an impressive and picturesque building, perched proudly on a rocky eminence. The interior is a veritable cornucopia of family portraits, antique furnishing, trophies and weapons. The most mysterious of all the castle's possessions hangs encased behind glass on one of the walls: a faded fragment of fragile yellow cloth that is known as the Fairy Flag.

Numerous legends have been woven around the origins of this curious relic. One tells how long, long ago a clan chieftain fell in love with a fairy princess and she with him. She asked her father for permission to marry him, but the king refused, saying that it would only break her heart since all mortals age and die. So upset was she that her father relented and consented to the union on condition that she return to her own people after a year and a day. The two were duly married, and before the year was up the princess had given birth to a son.

At the end of the allotted period the King of the Fairies arrived at Dunvegan to collect his daughter. She bade her husband farewell and made him promise that their child would never be left alone or be allowed to cry, since the sound of his tears would be impossible for her to bear. The chieftain sank into a fit of despondency and for months pined for his fairy bride.

Then, one day, the people of his clan attempted to lift his depression by holding a great feast. A maid had been assigned the task of watching over the infant, but such were the sounds of the revelry that she snuck away from her post to watch the entertainment. Whilst she was away, the boy began to cry and the sound carried all the way to Fairyland, where his mother heard it and immediately appeared at his crib. When the maid returned she was astonished to find her old mistress cradling the child in her arms, having wrapped him in her fairy shawl. The mother smiled, set the now sleeping child down, kissed him gently on the forehead and vanished. Years later, the boy revealed that his mother had told him that her shawl was a magic talisman and that, if ever the Macleods were in danger, they should wave it to summon the assistance of the fairy host, but it could only ever be used three times. Any more and disaster would befall the clan.

According to legend, its powers of enchantment have so far been used twice, but its protection has been sought in various other ways. Warriors are said to have cut squares from the fabric to carry as protection in battle and, during World War II, the young men of the clan are reputed to have kept pictures of the flag in their wallets while flying in the Battle of Britain, and not one of them was killed. In the dark days of that same conflict, the chief of the clan agreed to bring the flag to England and wave it from the cliffs of Dover should the Germans attempt an invasion.

LOCH NESS
The Loch Ness Monster
THE GREAT GLEN, HIGHLAND

Long ago there was no loch in the Great Glen; instead the 38.5 kilometres (24 miles) over which the waters of Loch Ness now stretch was a rich and fertile valley, dotted with an abundance of farms and homesteads. At the centre of this lush dale was a magic spring guarded by a strict taboo. Anyone who drew water from it must replace its cover the moment they had finished; failure to do so would blight the lives of those who lived in the vale. One day a woman had just begun filling her bucket when she heard her baby screaming in agony. Panicking, she left the spring uncovered and ran to assist. Immediately the well overflowed and a torrent of raging water cascaded behind her and flooded the valley. The inhabitants fled to the hills, crying as they went, 'Tha loch nis ann' ('There is a loch there now'), from which came the name Loch Ness.

Loch Ness lies at the northern end of the Great Glen, a geological fault that slashes across the Scottish Highlands. Its dark rippling water presents the wayfarer with an ever-changing panorama of hill, water and woodland. No one knows for certain exactly how deep this mysterious loch is, but its deepest and most sinister portion is that below the hollow shell of Urquhart Castle, beneath which, legend holds, exist underwater caves that are home to a colony of monsters. And of course Loch Ness, despite its stunning scenery, is best known for the enigmatic creature that is said to lurk beneath its peat-blackened waters, and whose forays to the surface have made it one of the world's most famous legendary beasts.

Whatever haunts the chilly depths of Loch Ness is neither a newcomer nor an idle legend to be derided out of hand. Indeed, the very first recorded encounter with either 'Nessie' or, more probably, one of her ancient ancestors, occurred in AD565 when a disciple of the Irish missionary, St Columba, was swimming across the River Ness to fetch a boat for his master. Suddenly a fearful beast appeared and, 'with a great roar and open mouth', rushed upon the swimmer. St Columba immediately made the sign of the cross and bellowed at the beast, 'Think not to go further, nor touch thou that man! Go back...' The monster obeyed and ever since, despite making regular appearances, it has never harmed anyone nor, for that matter, emitted even the slightest roar.

The modern interest in Nessie began with the opening of a main road along the north shore of the loch in 1933. In December of that year, a national newspaper sponsored the first endeavour to find the monster, by engaging the services of big game hunter Marmaduke Weatherall and photographer Gustav Pauli. Huge excitement was generated when, deep in the undergrowth by the side of the loch, the two discovered a large footprint, apparently left by a massive creature. Unfortunately this was soon revealed to have been a hoax, perpetrated with the aid of a dried hippopotamus foot, usually used as an umbrella stand!

ABOVE: Hugh Gray's photograph of the Loch Ness monster was taken on 12th November 1933 and is one of many that have helped make Nessie famous the world over.

BELOW: As well as containing Britain's greatest volume of fresh water, Loch Ness may also be home to the world's most famous and elusive monster.

Then, on 19th April 1934, Harley Street consultant Robert Kenneth Wilson took the famous 'surgeon's photograph' of a seemingly long-necked creature swimming across Loch Ness and gave the world its most enduring image of the fabled beast. Although his picture has been proved a fake, there have since been over 1,000 reported sightings. Disregarding proven hoaxes, mistaken identifications of natural objects, optical illusions, or wishful thinking – and it must be said that these can certainly account for a large proportion – there still remains sufficient evidence from sober, honest and publicity-shy witnesses, to suggest that something mysterious does indeed reside in Loch Ness.

Debate rages over the nature of the beast. Those who have seen the monster close up say that it is either slug- or eel-like with a head resembling that of a sheep or seal. Its length has been estimated at anywhere between 7.6–10.6 metres (25–35 feet), and its skin texture is described as 'warty' and 'slimy'. Some say that it is an unknown species of fish; others that it is a survivor from prehistoric times, possibly a plesiosaurus. Sceptics dismiss it as a mass of rotting vegetation, a group of frolicking water otters, a swimming deer, or even a sunken World War I zeppelin that periodically rises to the surface. Numerous scientific expeditions have failed to provide conclusive proof for its existence, and those photographers who hope to catch 'Nessie' on film have long grown used to her annoying habit of appearing when they are *sans* camera.

Whatever may or may not live beneath the waters of Britain's greatest volume of fresh water, its legend refuses to die, and visitors flock from all over the globe in the hope of catching a glimpse. Perhaps the final word should go to naturalist Dr David Bellamy, who said of Nessie, 'I hope it's there. But I hope they don't find it – because if they do, they'll do something nasty to it.'

CYDERHALL
Sigurd's Howe
NR DORNOCH, HIGHLAND

One of the most unusual legends of northern Scotland is connected with a farm, now called Cyderhall, situated on the road that runs between Meikle Ferry and Dornoch. Centuries ago this was known as Sigurd's Howe or 'Sigurd's burial mound', based on the tradition that Sigurd Eysteinsson – first Earl of Orkney – was buried here following his bizarre death in AD890.

Sigurd was a Norseman and ruler of Orkney by conquest. With the islands secure, his forces swept into the territories of Caithness and Sutherland, which were soon under Norse possession. Chief amongst those to resist the occupation was a Scottish earl by the name of Maelbrigte Tusk, so-called because of a prominent bucktooth that protruded in a grotesque fashion from his mouth.

The two nobles decided to settle their differences in open combat, and agreed to each bring 40 men to the battlefield. Sigurd, however, reneged on the deal and turned up with 80 soldiers mounted two each on his 40 horses. Seeing four pairs of legs astride each beast, Maelbrigte realized that his adversary had betrayed him but, all the same,

BELOW: Sigurd Eysteinsson died from an infected scratch on his leg, received from the tooth of the severed head of his enemy, Maelbrigte Tusk, that swung as he rode on his horse.

ordered his men to fight on. Despite their courageous stand the outnumbered Scots perished and Maelbrigte was slain. The elated Sigurd cut off his vanquished enemy's head and rode off with the grisly trophy swinging from his saddle.

At this point fate intervened to inflict a gloriously ironic twist of vengeance. As Sigurd galloped along, the jouncing head swung against him and Maelbrigte's tooth inflicted a deep scratch on his leg. The wound became infected and before long Earl Sigurd collapsed into a fevered delirium, died and was buried where he had fallen at a place they called Sigurd's Howe in his memory.

CULROSS ABBEY
Witches and Underground Tunnels
FIFE

The pretty and colourful town of Culross was the setting for a somewhat bizarre legend concerning a local witch named Helen Eliot. She had been sentenced to death and was about to be burnt at the stake when the Devil suddenly appeared and, scooping her up in his arms, carried her high into the air. Needless to say all who saw this demonic spectacle were awestruck, none more so than Helen Eliot herself who let out a screaming profanity to the effect of, 'Oh my God'. On hearing it, the Devil promptly dropped her, and she fell to the

ABOVE: Legend says that a hidden tunnel lies deep beneath Culross Abbey and it will lead intrepid seekers to a man in a golden chair. He will bestow great riches upon those who get to him without being killed first!

ground with such force that she 'did brake her leggs'. Unperturbed by the brief bout of demonic interference, the good citizens of Culross strapped her into a chair, carried her back to the stake and burnt her alive.

The town's Cistercian abbey was founded in 1217 and was dedicated to St Serf and St Mary. Dissolved during the Reformation, it is now mostly in ruins with the exception of the monks' choir, which has served as the parish church since 1633. Legend says that a tunnel runs deep beneath the abbey. In it sits a man in a golden chair waiting to bestow riches upon anyone that manages to find him. Those who may be tempted to venture in search of this underworld lottery should heed the fate of the blind piper who, accompanied by his little dog, descended into the vaults and set off through the subterranean labyrinth, playing a merry tune to enable those above ground to follow his progress. The pipes were heard as far as the West Kirk, almost a mile away, but they suddenly fell silent. Although the dog emerged, the piper was never seen again having, it was presumed, been taken by the demons that are known to lurk in this underground world of shadow.

FURTHER READING

Ashe, Geoffrey. *Mythology of the British Isles* (Methuen, 1990)

Atkinson, Tom. *The Empty Lands* (Luath Press, 1994)

Atkinson, Tom. *The Roads to the Isles* (Luath Press, 1994)

Begg, Paul; Fido, Martin and Skinner, Keith. *The Jack the Ripper A-Z* (Headline Book Publishing, 1996)

Berthelot, Anne. *King Arthur Chivalry and Legend* (Thames and Hudson, 1997)

Byrne, Tom. *Tales from the Past* (Iron Market Press, 1977)

Chambers, Anne, *Granuail* (Wolfhound Press, 1998)

Curan, Bob. *The Creatures of Celtic Myth* (Cassell and Co, 2000)

Dames, Michael. *Mythic Ireland* (Thames and Hudson, 1996)

Dashwood, Sir Francis. *The Dashwoods of West Wycombe* (Autrum Press, 1990)

Dixon, Mike. *Arthurian Myth and Legend* (Brockhampton Press, 1998)

Doel, Fran and Geoff. *Robin Hood, Outlaw or Greenwood Myth* (Tempus, 2000)

Evans, Hilary and Mary. *Hero on a Stolen Horse* (Book Club Associates, 1977)

Evans, Stewart P. and Skinner K. *Jack the Ripper, Letters from Hell* (Sutton Publishing, 2001)

Folklore, Myths and Legends of Britain (Readers Digest Association Ltd, 1977)

Gregory, Lady. *Irish Mythology* (Chancellor Press, 2000)

Home, Gordon. *Medieval London* (Bracken Books, 1994)

Holt, J.C. *Robin Hood* (Thames and Hudson, 1982)

Jones, Richard. *England's Favorite Cities* (Macmillan, 1994)

Jones, Richard. *Haunted Britain and Ireland* (New Holland, 2001)

Jones, Richard. *Memorable Walks in London* (4th ed. Hungry Minds, 2001)

Jones, Richard. *That's Magic* (New Holland, 2001)

Jones, Richard. *Walking Haunted London* (New Holland, 1999)

Mason, John. *Haunted Heritage* (Collins and Brown, 1999)

McHardy, Stuart. *Scotland: Myth, Legend and Folklore* (Luath Press, 1999)

Neeson, Eoin. *Celtic Myths and Legends* (Mercier Press, 1998)

Ross, Anne. *Folklore of Wales* (Tempus Publishing, 2001)

Scott, Reginald. *The Discoverie of Witchcraft* (Dover, 1972)

Simpson, Jacqueline and Roud, Steve. *A Dictionary of English Folklore* (Oxford University Press, 2000)

Slavin, Michael. *The Book of Tara* (Wolfhound Press, 1996)

Swire, Otta F. *The Highlands and their Legends* (Oliver and Boyd, 1963)

Turner, Mark. *Folklore and Mysteries of the Cotswolds* (Robert Hale, 1993)

Wales, Tony. *A Treasury of Sussex Folklore* (S.B. Publications, 2000)

Westwood, Jennifer. *Albion, A Guide to Legendary Britain* (Book Club Associates, 1986)

Zaczek, Iain. *The Book of Irish Legends* (Cico Books, 2001)

INDEX

ACKNOWLEDGEMENTS

The research for this book has taken me all over Britain and Ireland, and numerous people have generously contributed their time and ideas to the project. Staff at local libraries helped me locate the sites and legends in their locale. People at castles, landmarks, even local service stations were always willing to proffer opinion and point me in the right direction. To others I was just a voice on the end of a telephone, trying to confirm dates and facts. To all of you I offer my sincere thanks.

At New Holland Publishers, I would like to thank Jo Hemmings and Lorna Sharrock for their encouragement, and Alan Marshall, whose evocative design is always such a pleasure to see. I would like to thank John Mason for his magnificent photography, and both him and author Phil Rickman for their many excellent suggestions.

I would like to thank my sister Geraldine Hennigan for being there whenever I needed to test out a story, and my wife Joanne without whose patient understanding I would have been lost. A big thank you also to my sons Thomas and William who showed admirable interest for a two- and a four-year-old as they plodded patiently around with me!

Publisher's Acknowledgements

All photographs by John Mason except for the following:

Dr PMJ Crook: page 42.

Fortean Picture Library: pages 30(b), 64(c), 76(b), 114(b), 142(t).

Mary Evans Picture Library: pages 86, 89, 115, 135(b); James Doyle: page 67(b); Hugh Gray: page 153(t); Tom Morgan: page 52; Lucy Pringle: page 27; Arthur Rackham Collection: page 51; N. C. Wyeth: page 10.

(t= top; b=bottom; c=centre; l=left; r=right)

While every effort has been taken to ensure that all suppliers of photographs have been credited, New Holland Publishers would like to apologise for any errors or omissions that may have occurred.